The Promise

D1292979

NCMC
BV
3265.2
.J33
1994

3040 2228

The Promise

The Story of Ed and Virginia Jacober

"The poor and needy search for water, but there is none; their tongues are parched with thirst. But I the LORD will answer them; I, the God of Israel, will not forsake them." (Isaiah 41:17)

"For he will command his angels concerning you to guard you in all your ways." (Psalm 91:11)

"I am with you and will watch over you wherever you go, and I will bring you back to this land. I will not leave you until I have done what I have promised you." (Genesis 28:15)

Virginia Jacober

Christian Publications

CAMP HILL, PENNSYLVANIA

Christian Publications
3825 Hartzdale Drive, Camp Hill, PA 17011

The mark of ✝ *vibrant faith*

ISBN: 0-87509-547-X
LOC Catalog Card Number: 93-74546
© 1994 by Christian Publications
All rights reserved
Printed in the United States of America

94 95 96 97 98   5 4 3 2 1

Cover illustration
© 1994, Karl Foster

Unless otherwise indicated, Scripture taken from the
HOLY BIBLE: NEW INTERNATIONAL VERSION,
© Copyright 1973, 1978, 1984 by the International Bible
Society. Used by permission of Zondervan Bible Publishers

Dedication

To all Alliance men and women,
friends and relatives
who faithfully
encouraged and supported us
financially, materially
and spiritually
through prayer.

Acknowledgments

My sincere appreciation to:

H. Robert Cowles, editor of *The Alliance Life*, who in the late 1950s printed the first article I sent from India. He encouraged me to continue writing. I did.

Friends I met on deputational tours who said, "You owe it to the Alliance to write up these stories you tell." I did.

Bill Brailey, who put the manuscript on his computer. To him I am deeply grateful for his help and advice.

The leadership of The Christian and Missionary Alliance. It has been a privilege to serve the Lord under their direction. They have made the recording of these experiences possible. To God be the glory!

Israel

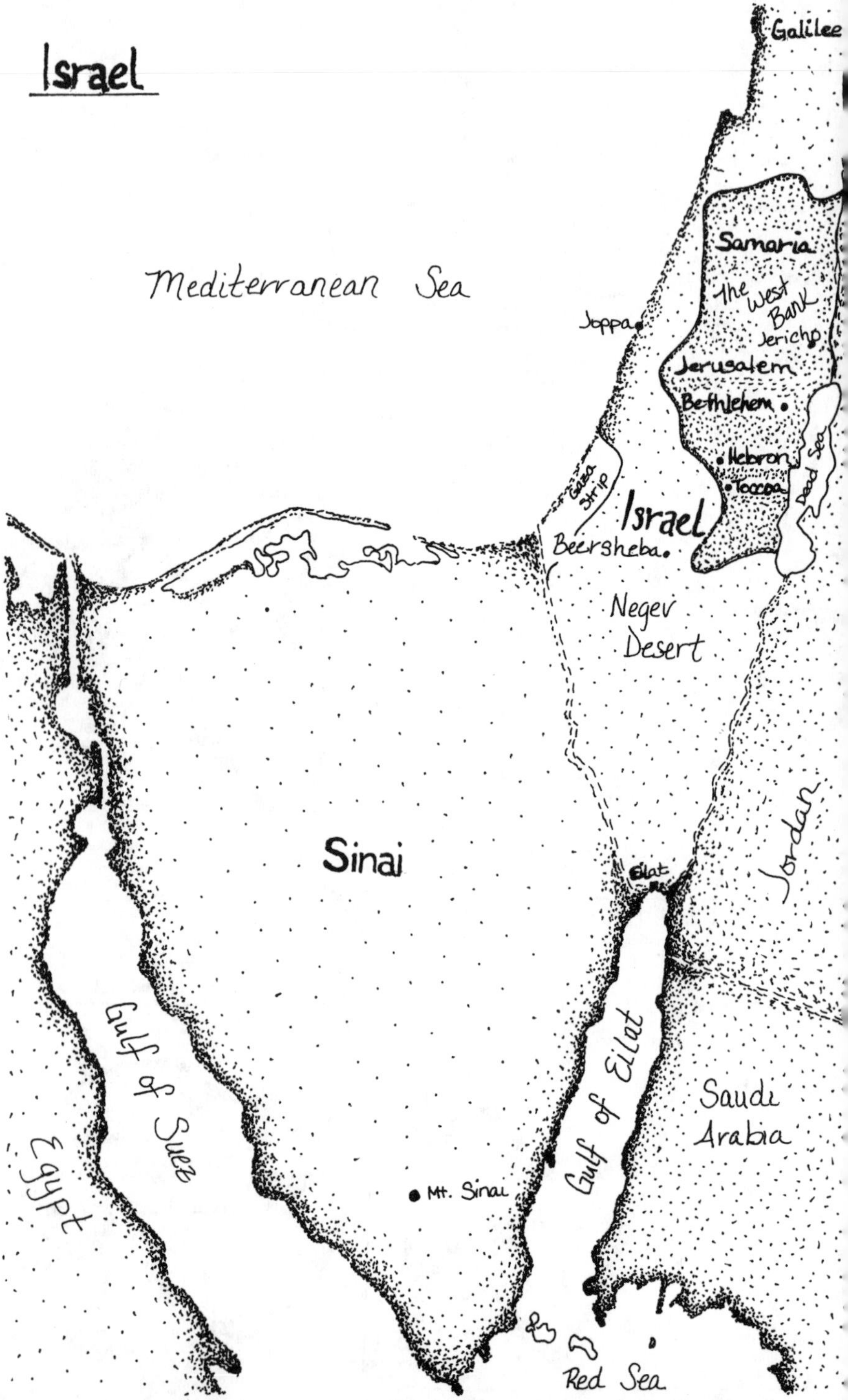
Galilee
Mediterranean Sea
Samaria
The West Bank
Joppa
Jericho
Jerusalem
Bethlehem
Hebron
Tocoa
Dead Sea
Gaza Strip
Israel
Beersheba
Negev Desert
Sinai
Elat
Jordan
Gulf of Suez
Gulf of Eilat
Saudi Arabia
Egypt
Mt. Sinai
Red Sea

Contents

1

God Had Other Plans

Most girls dream of a fairy-tale romance. I certainly did. But I had no idea that mine would begin at a youth meeting sponsored by the Burns Avenue Christian and Missionary Alliance Church in Dayton, Ohio where I lived.

I was a senior in high school and was making plans to attend Nyack College. In fact, it was our shared interest in Nyack that had prompted Jean Smith to invite me to the meeting.

The tall, dark and handsome Edward Jacober had just graduated from Worcester Polytechnic Institute in Massachusetts with a degree in mechanical engineering. His first job, for the government, had brought him just weeks before from his home in Newark, New Jersey, to work at Wright-Patterson Air Force Base.

Not long after his arrival church friends invited him along on a trip to visit the Moody Bible Institute in Chicago. There he purchased a book written by Clarence Larkin, an engineer like himself. The detailed charts appealed to

Ed's mathematical mind.

One evening he was lying in bed reading this fascinating book when four words caught his attention: "Christ died for you." He rolled out of bed onto his knees and prayed, "Thank You, Lord, for dying for me. Now what can I do for You?" He went out and bought a Bible and launched into a systematic study of various Bible correspondence courses.

We began dating, and Ed told me later that when he saw me walk through the door at the youth meeting he said to himself, *That's the girl I'm going to marry!* His intentions were increasingly supported by flowers, corsages, candy, gifts and expensive restaurant dinners.

My ambition as a young girl was to become a nurse. However, when I was 14 I heard a missionary speak at Beulah Beach Conference on Lake Erie and I knew that night God wanted me to be a missionary. I did not see a vision or hear a voice, but after Mary Dixon related her experiences in Borneo I returned to the little tent where I was staying, knelt on the straw beside my army cot and prayed, "All right, Lord, if this is what You want me to do, I'll do it. I won't be a nurse. I'll be a missionary." I did not know then that the two could be combined. But I had made a promise and I intended to keep it.

People began to ask me what mission field I was going to. I could not give them an answer. I did not know myself. I was interested in

Borneo because that was where Mary Dixon was working. The phrase, "To Nyack, then to the Dyak" sounded logical to me.

But God had other plans.

During a summer vacation, the church asked me to chaperone a group of young people to the youth camp at Beulah Beach. One afternoon during devotions a verse in Isaiah caught my attention: "The poor and needy search for water, but there is none; their tongues are parched with thirst. But I the LORD will answer them; I, the God of Israel, will not forsake them" (41:17).

I saw a vision of a man staggering across a desert, and I believed he was an Arab. The verse and the vision became God's call to me, a call that would take me on a life's path that could be designed only by one so all-knowing and all-loving as the Master Designer Himself.

I hungrily began to devour whatever information I could find about Arab culture and religion, and gradually my love for Arabs grew until it became a deep, intense desire to live and work with them. I set my face toward the Near East.

But right now I had a life-changing decision to make.

As soon as I graduated from high school Ed asked me to marry him. Of course I wanted to be married, and to be proposed to by a handsome professional who loved her was any teenage girl's romantic dream come true.

I felt, however, that it was a temptation to turn me aside from keeping my promise to God and doing what I knew He wanted me to do. I was determined to obey the Lord. No one and nothing would deter me from following His plan for my life. I clung to the vow I had made.

"Sorry," I told Ed with wisdom perhaps beyond my years, "you're an engineer and I'm going to be a missionary. We'll just have to wait and see how the Lord works it out."

Jean and I went to Nyack in the fall of 1942. One day the dean of women called Jean, who was now my dear friend and roommate, and me into her office and asked us if we would like to take a medical course for missionaries in New York City.

I was delighted. God was giving me back the very thing I had surrendered to Him and now I was getting training that would prove useful on the mission field: how to treat fevers, parasites, burns, infections and to practice dentistry and midwifery. I didn't know then that someday I would deliver and even name babies—an exciting and awesome responsibility.

Every time I returned home for holidays or the summer Ed proposed again. He proposed so often I lost count. And always, I gave him the same answer.

One day a letter came from Ed saying he had heard a missionary speak at a conference and had committed his life to the Lord for overseas service. I was delighted! God, it seemed, was working out His plan to bring us together to serve Him. Our relationship took on a new and deeper significance.

World War II interrupted our lives but not our romance. V-mail, as it was called, became our lifeline. When the war ended, Ed's name was way down on the list for returning from Europe to the States. We were disappointed—it could take months before he would be eligible to come home.

But once again God had other plans and He intervened in a most miraculous way.

During his engineering days, Ed's department in the government had placed a contract with a businessman who was later charged with embezzling. Ed was called to be a witness in the court case, but by the time he arrived in the States the case had been dismissed. A short time later he was discharged from the army.

Instead of returning to the engineering job which was waiting for him at the base, Ed enrolled at Dallas Theological Seminary to study for a Master's degree in theology.

By this time I had completed four years (including some medical courses) at Nyack. When I saw that Ed was setting aside his profession and the potentially lucrative career it promised to train for missionary service, I agreed to marry him.

2

On Our Way

We pastored the Alliance church in Dallas, Texas, while Ed attended seminary. During his senior year our first baby, Ruth, was born, a delightful blessing to us both. As Ed carried her around he crooned the words of an old song: "A little bit of heaven came to our house to stay."

When he graduated we applied to the board for foreign service. Our choice was the Middle East—among the Arabs who were so dear to my heart—but the board informed us that missionaries were urgently needed in India.

We accepted the appointment, believing it was God's plan for us even though I wondered to myself how it fit with the intense love I believed God had given me for Arabs and Muslims many years earlier. The answer to that question would not be long in coming.

Raising the money for our first year's support seemed like an insurmountable barrier. Our little church was willing but unable to handle such an amount. The problem loomed large on our horizon.

One day we received a Western Union telegram from the church in Dayton: "First year support pledged stop make plans to come to Dayton early stop Rev. Carl R. Bennett." It was an answer to prayer.

Now all we had to do was pass a rigorous physical examination. We were shocked with the results—I was too thin! Ed was too fat! And my blood count was not high enough.

We began an unusual regimen: I swallowed iron pills and Ed took appetite curbers. I gorged on rich foods and guzzled gallons of half-'n'-half while Ed stuffed himself with huge bowls of shredded cabbage.

After a year, we finally balanced the scales satisfactorily: Ed had lost 20 pounds and I had gained almost as many. Confidently we wrote to the medical board. Their reply was unnerving. Since a year had passed, they said, we would have to take another set of examinations.

We walked into the doctor's office only somewhat optimistically. *Surely all our labors of the past year will not be in vain*, I tried to assure myself. *But what if we still don't meet the requirements? What if we still are unable to go?*

The results of the blood test were surprising! My blood was right where it had been the year before but, explained the doctor, this was normal for women living in the South. In our hearts we knew that his explanation would not be accepted by the medical board in New York. We were so disappointed we picked up the blank exam forms and walked out.

At home we knelt beside the sofa and began to pray. Sometime later we rose to our feet with a renewed assurance that God had called us to go overseas. We—and He—would not let anything hinder us.

One sleepless night I had a vision of people—thousands of them—whose blood would be upon my hands if I failed to tell them about Jesus. The Scripture confirmed the reality of this impression: "When I say to the wicked, 'O wicked man, you will surely die,' and you do not speak out to dissuade him from his ways, that wicked man will die for his sin, and I will hold you accountable for his blood" (Ezekiel 33:8).

As we prayed, God inspired us with faith to believe that He could do the impossible. Popping a couple of iron pills into my mouth, I suggested we try another doctor. The blood test taken, we waited to see what God would do.

When the report arrived the count was exactly where the medical board required it. We had passed the entire examination!

Coincidence? A difference in testing technique? No. We checked later with a hematologist who assured us that under normal circumstances such a thing could not happen. God did it! He showed us that there is no limit to the possibilities which faith may claim, especially when He Himself plants His faith in our hearts.

One step of faith led to another. Our visas

had not yet been granted. We prayed and we waited. After three long months they finally arrived.

Last-minute berths on a freighter were booked for Ed and me and Ruthy who was now two years old. Gazing out over the dark, rough Atlantic, I fought a persistent childhood fear of water and death by drowning. Six weeks of this icy-cold, blue-black ocean loomed forbiddingly in my mind. I decided to take my fear to the only One who could help me and soon I was actually enjoying the feel of gently swaying decks and salt spray on my lips.

One day, busy ironing in the cabin, I suddenly noticed that quiet little Ruthy was missing. Knowing that the widely spaced rails of the ship gave scant protection for curious and adventuresome toddlers, I hurried out on deck, inwardly frantic but outwardly trying to appear calm.

I finally found her perched contentedly on the bottom rail with her fingers wrapped around the middle one and her legs dangling out over the sea. A lump arose in my throat as I surveyed the rain-slicked deck and rails. One slip could have plunged her into the water.

I called to her in what I hoped was a normal tone of voice that would betray none of the panic I was feeling. She turned and smiled innocently as I reached out my hand and helped her back across the deck to safety. How I thanked God for giving little children spe-

cial guardian angels and for Christians back
home who I knew were praying for us.

Three terrible storms—one each in the
Atlantic, the Mediterranean and the Indian
Ocean—played havoc with the cargo of auto-
mobiles cabled onto the decks of the ship.
Below deck silverware slid off the screwed-
down dining room tables and china crashed
to the floor. Passengers stumbled dizzily along
the narrow passageways.

When the terrible rock-and-roll escalated to
violent up-and-down motion I began imitating
it: up to the bathroom, down to the bed as my
meals went in reverse motion. Ed, on the other
hand, loved it all and gladly accepted the stew-
ard's invitation to raid the galley refrigerator
night after night. Ironically, by the time we
reached India, I had lost my hard-earned
pounds and Ed had regained his. We were both
back to normal once again!

The ship carried only nine passengers and all
nine were missionaries. At first the captain
insisted that this was bad luck, but when a
crew member was injured in an accident, he
was relieved that one of us, a nurse, could tend
the man until we reached the Azores where
he was put ashore. As a result of this incident,
the chief engineer heard Ed's testimony and
came to know Christ as his Savior.

As we approached the west coast of Arabia, I
had visions of deserts and camels, horsemen
and tents, flowing robes and headdresses.

Instead, from our porthole we could see only the small town of Jiddah and a harem of women arriving at the dock in the back of a Ford pick-up.

Taking advantage of this opportunity to meet some real Arabs, we decided to go talk with them. We managed to communicate with gestures and facial expressions and the women were particularly entranced by Ruthy. As we turned to leave they kissed their fingers and touched them to her forehead.

My heart followed them as they drove away. Was this where I belonged?

I was soon to discover that there were over 50 million Muslims in India. Some of them would become our dearest friends.

3

Blood, Sweat and Tears

It was dawn when the coast of the city of Bombay first appeared through the mist. But by the time we disembarked, the sun was blazing.

An overnight train took us 300 miles northwest to Ahmedabad, the capital of the state of Gujarat, which was to become our new home. Hundreds of noisy myna birds, perched on the steel rafters of the railway station, greeted us with deafening chatter. The local missionaries, Louis and Esther King, Betty Dyke and Ruth Brabazon welcomed us warmly along with a group of Indian Christians who sang their special welcome.

Getting acquainted with this ancient and enchanting land was both shocking and pleasureable. Each evening we continued a family habit of taking a walk before sunset. I was appalled to see hundreds of red splashes on the sidewalks and in the gutters.

"The people are dying of tuberculosis," I remarked to Ed. "Conditions are worse than I imagined."

I was about to learn that the ugly red blotches were not blood—they were betel nut juice! A green leaf is wrapped around ground lime and then chewed like tobacco. In the process it all turns blood-red and the juice is spit.

Temples were everywhere. A little cement one beneath a stand of trees contained the remnants of a bird's wing, leg and foot. Another shrine housed a silver-painted image to which offerings of fruits, flowers and money were given.

Kali, the goddess of blood and death, had her own temple. Coconut sellers lined up in front of the huge, elaborately decorated edifice with their carts piled high so that worshipers could present an offering. The black statue wore a necklace of the skulls of the 40 husbands she had murdered. Her enlarged red tongue dripped blood—an offering she sometimes required for the forgiveness of sin.

One newspaper reported that a zealous young man had cut his finger and let the blood drip onto Kali. Then, in a frenzy, he had cut his throat, committing suicide.

Even more shocking were the murders committed by those who claimed that in a dream Kali told them to offer the blood of a human to appease her wrath and merit her favor.

We read that even small children were kidnapped and offered in sacrifice to Kali's demands. A brother and sister were decapitated by a couple who wanted to have a child, their bodies thrown into a well, their heads offered on a platter to the goddess.

A young boy was lured away from home by the promise of candy. After eating the drug-laced sweets, he became unconscious, was tied up, his body cut and the blood dripped onto a bowl of rice. A group of men then ate the blood-soaked rice believing it would give them good luck, strength and youth.

Surely these people needed desperately to hear about the love of One who centuries ago had shed His blood on the cross as a payment for *all* sin. His sacrifice made all others unnecessary.

>─┼◆─○─◆┼─◁

During World War II, Prime Minister Churchill declared that victory must be won by "blood, sweat and tears." Newspaper articles and visits to the temples had already introduced us to blood. Now we were about to sweat!

The day we arrived at the mission station, our senior missionaries asked, "When do you want to begin learning the language?"

With more zeal than wisdom we answered, "Tomorrow."

They promptly sent word to the teacher and at eight o'clock the next morning a card table and chairs were set up in the lovely compound garden. Without unpacking our suitcases or opening our trunks, we sat down with our instructor who, we soon discovered, knew even less about teaching Gujarati than we did about learning it.

Bloody-looking betel nut juice trickled over his stained lips and down the corners of his nearly toothless mouth. At one point, wanting a visual demonstration of how to pronounce a certain sound, I knelt down in front of the old man to see where his bright red tongue was placed. Much to my chagrin I lost my balance and nearly toppled into his lap!

We soon learned how to flip our tongue from the roof of our mouths and to make lip, tooth, palatal, guttural and nasal sounds we had never heard, much less experienced before.

Our mistakes were both embarrassing and hilarious. A button was missing from Ruthy's dress and I wanted to tell the ayah (the nursemaid, housecleaner and wash woman combined) that it might be in my sewing box. The phrase came out, "Perhaps the button is in my stomach." Sumie's gentle smile revealed my error.

Our cook was amused when I asked him to bring the butter because by using breath with a syllable which should be spoken without breath, I had unwittingly ordered, "Please bring me a bedbug." Later, we had plenty of bedbugs without even asking for them!

After six weeks we were sent to a language school directed by one of our own missionaries, Myra Wing. Her patience and courage rubbed off on us. She believed we would learn to read, write and speak the Gujarati language. Under her inspiration we began to believe it, too.

The highlight of our stay at the school came one day when Ed spoke through a translator to the boys at the boarding school. One young teenager came forward to accept Christ. This was why we were in India—to win people to Christ! We felt like celebrating!

The Mission arranged for us, along with John and Leona Garrison and Betty Dyke, to escape the awful heat of the lowlands by going to the Himalaya mountains for six months of study. "Fairview," the appropriately named Alliance bungalow, overlooked snow-covered peaks jutting into the clouds 50 miles in the distance. Nearer, rows of tree-laden ranges were dotted with bright red rhododendron blossoms.

One morning we were concentrating in class. In the yard outside the window the two children, our Ruth and the Garrison's son David, were playing under the care of their ayahs. Suddenly we saw the women and the watchman run toward the open gate. We sprang to our feet as the cook came to the door to announce that the children were missing!

We all dispersed in different directions, our imaginations projecting visions of those two two-year-olds tumbling hundreds of feet down any one of the steep cliffs which dotted the area.

Much to our relief, the watchman found the

runaways with their tiny hands gripping the metal railings overlooking a 12-foot precipice. Once again, we thanked God for the loving protection of guardian angels and the prayers of faithful Christians back home.

＞—┼—◆＞—○—＜◆—┼—＜

It was the night before we were scheduled to take our second year language exams. We planned to get up at five a.m. in order to catch a bus that would take us to the central station where we would board a second bus to our destination.

For several months Ruthy had been troubled with a seemingly endless stream of problems: measles, worms, head lice, a lung infection which required 10 days of injections, and blood poisoning from stubbing her toe on a cow dung and mud floor. Now, she came down with a severe tonsillitis attack. Her fever began climbing one degree for every hour that passed.

Instead of working on last-minute brushing-up for the exam, I stayed by her bed, bathing her face and periodically taking her temperature. By one o'clock in the morning I was desperate. I knelt beside her and prayed, "Oh God, please make this fever subside for her sake as well as mine. I cannot leave a sick baby nor can I cope with that oral interview a few hours from now unless I get some sleep."

Within an hour the fever began to drop and we both rested. God had answered prayer. I knew He was watching over our child and I felt

His presence as the bus rattled along the quiet streets at dawn that morning.

I passed the exam. And Ed did, too.

The dictionary says the archaic expression for "sweat" means "hard work"—a truly apt description of language study!

>-+-+>-+-O-+<-+-+-<

The following year our second baby, Daniel, was born. The Indians—and we—were delighted that we had a son! Indian parents desire at least one son to carry on the family name and care for them in their old age—a kind of social security.

Danny was just a few months old when we were appointed to live and work in the village of Dhandhuka and the hundreds of villages surrounding it. The compound was extensive: there was a school and church, the missionary bungalow and a line of rooms like a motel which housed the pastor, evangelist, teacher, Bible woman, cook, watchman and their families. The well behind our bungalow supplied water for washing, but drinking water had to be carried across the fields from the railway station.

Ed immediately began village evangelism and literature distribution plus a Bible teaching ministry which sometimes took him away from home for days at a time.

With a new baby, my activities were limited but they included a weekly women's meeting, a daily clinic for the children of the compound and accompanying Edna, the Bible woman, who taught adult literacy and did house-to-house visitation.

During the monsoons when roads were utterly impassable, we concentrated on our immediate area. It was there that we met two Muslim women—Helima and Jerdi. At last God was allowing me to minister to the people I loved. I prayed and wept and believed that He would use me to lead these two women and many other Muslims to Christ.

Helima lived next door to a Christian woman, Ganga, whom we were teaching to read and write in Gujarati. Edna and I went to Ganga's home every morning for a lesson and Helima would often drop by to chat.

One day Helima's son got into an argument with a friend over some debts. In his depression he tried to commit suicide by throwing kerosene on his shirt and setting himself on fire. His attempt was unsuccessful and for several weeks I treated his badly burned back and arms until they healed.

Another day at Ganga's place Helima invited us to come and see her new grandson who had been born just hours before. Ignoring the flies and the oppressive humidity, we got up from the cow dung floor where we had been having the lesson and followed Helima to her small room.

I picked up the tiny child and ran my fingers over his soft, silky-black hair.

"You are different than we are," Helima suddenly remarked, shattering the magic of the moment.

"I can't change the color of my skin," I replied, "but Jesus loves us all equally." A door of witness with Helima was slowly opening.

Later I gave the baby a little jacket and Helima, in return, brought me a gift—a bag full of vegetables. It was a seal of our friendship.

When the baby was a few weeks old he became ill. Helima and the mother brought him to me for medical help and expressed their gratitude for the time and concern I showed.

"I have done this because of love. Jesus says, 'Love one another as I have loved you.' " And then I added quickly, "Shall I pray for your baby?"

They did not object so I put my hand on the little one.

"Oh, Lord Jesus," I prayed, "stretch out Your hand and make this baby well."

When I looked up, the women's lips were quivering, their eyes brimming with tears.

The next day the baby was well.

"He hasn't cried at all and he's been sleeping," the grateful mother said.

"We prayed, didn't we?" I pressed.

One day I heard that Helima was sick so I tramped across the fields to her house. I found her with a high fever and a hacking cough. Her parchment-like skin hung loosely over her fragile frame.

"I'm dying," she moaned as I entered the

house.

Convinced that she might be right I replied, "Then you should get ready." Again I told her that if she believed and accepted Jesus He would cleanse the sin from her heart and she would be ready to go and live with Him.

Mustering her strength she turned toward me.

"When you came to teach Ganga next door and I heard the story of Jesus for the first time joy came into my heart," she said weakly. I was happy to hear that, but had such a response led to believing faith? I wasn't sure.

Helima recovered, but she never made a public declaration of her faith in Christ. That would have involved much opposition and persecution from her own people.

Dr. Samuel Zwemer, famous missionary to the Muslims, believed that in the resurrection many Christians would rise from Muslim graves.

I think so, too. I hope that Helima will be one of them.

>–+–‹›–O–‹›–+–‹

A little wrinkled old woman named Jerdi, another Muslim, lay tucked away in a room on the far side of our village. Crippled with arthritis, she had been confined to her rope cot for four years. She could neither raise her head nor sit up unless someone helped her. If anyone entered her bare little room she could only look out of the corner of her eye to see who was there. No one cared for her except her

son who came occasionally to visit and a neighbor's child who somtimes ran errands for her.

Edna found Jerdi one day as she was passing
through her neighborhood. She asked me if I
would like to go and meet her.

It had rained during the night, turning the
fields into lakes and the streets into filthy pud-
dles of trash and manure. Placing Danny on my
hip and taking off my sandals, I followed Edna
through the fields of muddy water that reached
nearly up to our knees. Finally at the road,
we hired a horse and buggy—the village taxi.

Arriving at Jerdi's doorway we called, "Hello,
how are you, Grandmother? Are you well?"

"Come in," Jerdi responded. "Who is it asking after my health?"

Jerdi's son Mohammed invited us to sit down
on a mattress on the floor. A crowd of neighbor
men, women and children flocked around to
stare at the foreigners. Danny's bright blond
hair, fair skin and use of the Gujarati language
were always an attraction.

Edna and I sang a song and preached to the
crowd. Then Mohammed told them to go home
so we could visit with his mother. After serving
us tea he left to go to work.

"How you must love me to take a horse and
buggy all this distance to come and see me!"
Jerdi exclaimed.

"Yes, Grandmother, that is true," we agreed.
"But Jesus loves you even more than we do."

I sat down on the edge of the cot and showed

her the colored pages of the Wordless Book, holding it close so she could see them. When I explained that the black page represented a sinful heart, Jerdi began to weep.

"It is like my sins," she cried. She had been a Hindu but many years before she had gone to live with a Muslim man.

"Oh yes, I am a sinner," she admitted.

I turned to the red page representing Jesus' blood that was shed on the cross. Jerdi repeated the Bible verse I quoted: "The blood of Jesus, his Son, purifies us from all sin" (1 John 1:7). And then, to my surprise, thoughtfully and with spiritual insight, she said, "Jesus' blood cleanses me from lying and cheating and stealing," naming her own sins.

As I began to explain the white page, a smile broke across her face, an outward expression of the inward transformation she had just experienced.

The last color was gold for heaven. That, too, she easily understood. With a clean heart she could go to live with God in heaven.

On the way home I did not notice the dirt that accummulated on my feet. I was walking on air. A Muslim woman had found Christ!

The next time we visited Jerdi, she repeated the verses and sang the songs we had taught her, adding some of her own lyrics. It was obvious that God's Word was taking root in her heart.

The cold weather was coming when we made

our last visit and Jerdi was having more arthrit-
ic pain.

"I wish I could go to be with the Lord," she
said. "If He would take me now, I am ready.
But I am afraid."

"You don't need to be afraid," I assured her.
"Jesus will be with you."

Jerdi lay with tears streaming out of the corners of her eyes.

"I will never forget Jesus, never forget, never
forget. I will not let His name loose from my
heart," she declared victoriously.

My agonizing tears in prayer for Jerdi and
others without Christ were being turned into
tears of joy!

4

The Dogs of Vadia

From the window beside my desk, I gazed across cotton fields and cactus fences to a tiny village of cow dung huts called Vadia. Some of the children from that village attended the one-room school on our compound. I talked to the teacher about holding a Bible class for the children, but he said it could not be arranged during school time.

Undaunted, I persisted. "Why not go to their village in the morning before they leave for school at 11 o'clock?"

"You can't go there," he answered. "The dogs are vicious and they bite. We saw a girl with a big chunk out of her leg where one of those dogs bit her."

"Let's pray that the Lord will let those dogs die," I responded somewhat bravely.

Still sensing a burden for Vadia I approached Edna about going.

"Oh, the dogs of that village are terrible," she said. "I went once and the people said the dogs bite. It isn't safe. Even the mailman won't go there."

I decided to write a letter to America asking

for prayer that God would intervene so we could go to Vadia. The answer came back saying that the Alliance Women were praying for our safe entrance into the village. One woman was even praying that God would smite the dogs!

I felt encouraged to go and "spy out the land" as Caleb and Joshua had done. So one evening before sundown Ed, Danny and I went for a walk in search of a path to Vadia. Though it was the monsoon season, there had been no rain for several days and the narrow footpath was fairly dry and negotiable. At first we followed a small ridge, but when we crossed the wet fields, mud stuck to our shoes until our feet became so heavy we could hardly lift them.

We could hear a few dogs barking in the distance. Yes, this was the way to Vadia. Now that we had found the path we turned toward home.

A young boy was herding a few oxen just ahead of us. I was walking in front carrying the baby when suddenly one of the oxen saw me and began running toward us. I stopped in my tracks, petrified.

The massive weight, pounding hoofs and long, curved and pointed horns of the ox were nearly upon me. Ed, whose reflexes did not petrify but electrify, grabbed me and with one arm swept Danny and me off the path and out into the field. The ox turned to follow and again Ed pushed us away. I stumbled and screamed. The baby began to cry.

Then it was over. Having chased us off his territory, the animal calmly sauntered back to join the rest of the herd.

We recognized this incident as a trick of our enemy Satan to discourage us from entering Vadia. But being determined, as all missionaries have to be to get to the field in the first place, the frightening experience only served to deepen my desire to reach those children with the gospel.

Again I spoke to Edna about starting the class in Vadia and again she mentioned the dreadful dogs. I told her that the women at home were praying for God to destroy them.

"We can be like Daniel going into the lions' den," I said encouragingly. "God's angel can shut the mouths of those dogs just as he did the lions'."

Finally Edna was convinced and we arranged to go. The monsoons were not over as we had thought and the day before we were scheduled to go, there was a terrible downpour. The path was washed out in some places, and although we waded in mud up to our shoe laces, my heart was singing a song of praise to God. At last we were on our way to Vadia!

"Madam Sahib," Edna said as we tramped along, "three days ago the pastor and the evangelist came through this village and they said there was not a child to be seen. All of them have gone to the fields to work with their parents."

"Oh well," I responded, "we shall see when
we get there." *Is this another attempt of the enemy
to discourage us?* I wondered to myself and to the
Lord.

We could hear the dogs barking as we
approached the village. A man living in a hut
on the outskirts saw us and offered to accompany us. Picking up a bamboo stick, he walked
ahead like a protective shield sent by the Lord
to make us aware of His presence.

Edna saw some dogs and asked nervously,
"Will those dogs bite?"

The man shook his head.

"No, they won't bite." His confidence was
only somewhat reassuring.

We walked up to a gray-haired man and his
wife who were sitting on a bed outside their hut
and explained why we had come—to teach the
children a song and tell them a story. They
welcomed us and pulled out a rope bed for us
to sit on. I knew what that meant: three days of
wildly itching bedbug bites on my legs! But
politeness forbade my refusal of their kindness.

The children were there, not out in the fields
as we had heard, and about 30 gathered around
us as we sang a tune familiar to them but with
words about Jesus living in the temple of our
hearts. The hostess sang along with us and her
husband urged the children to participate.

We told a flannelgraph story and taught them
a Scripture verse. To each one who would stand
and recite the verse we gave a used greeting

card. Their eyes shone with delight as they reached out grubby hands for the brightly colored reward.

And, to our amazement and relief, not one dog even barked while we were there!

A few hours later we waded back home with the blistering sun causing rivulets of sweat to pour down our faces and drip off the end of our noses. My clothes clung to me but I didn't care. I praised God for this victory over the enemy and his efforts to hinder our work.

The next week we went to Vadia again. As we entered the village several dogs were lying in the grass apparently asleep. We quietly slipped past. Another dog barked but a little boy chased it away with a stick.

Again Edna asked, "Will that dog bite?"

"No, it won't bite," the child replied.

Thirty-five children gathered this time. Some of them even remembered the verse they had learned the week before.

While we were drinking tea I questioned one of the mothers.

"What happened to the biting dogs?"

"Oh, those dogs are dead," she replied nonchalantly.

As we were leaving we looked closely at the dogs lying in the grass. She was right—they were dead.

A couple of months later we were met at the edge of the village by five dogs. One was a huge black mean-looking mongrel. The people

told us it had bitten a little girl. The villagers
chased the dogs away so we could have our
meeting, and later the little girl's father brought
her to the mission so I could "do medicine" for
her. There were five wounds on her leg, one of
them raw and open to the bone. For two weeks
I treated and bandaged it daily.

On one of these visits an older boy from the
village came along with the little girl.

"When you come to Vadia the next time," he
advised, "bring a stick with you. The men of
the village are going to kill the black dog but
they haven't done it yet."

Edna and I prayed for protection as we started out. Some children playing outside the village offered to walk in front of us to keep the
dogs away, and every week thereafter the Lord
had someone at the edge of the village ready to
escort us.

The black dog never came around but it kept
on biting and I kept on treating its victims.
The women in America who were praying about
the biting dogs were the same ones who had
torn up old sheets and rolled them into the
bandages I was using to wrap around the
wounds inflicted by those dogs.

We had been having a good ministry with the
children and now slowly, almost impercepti-
bly, we were gaining the confidence of Vadia's
women. They came to admire our new baby,
Jimmy, and to sing our Christian songs. Soon
they were visiting us regularly, bringing their

babies with sore eyes, infections and more children with bites. One day, because they could
not pronounce my English name, they gave me
an Indian one—Merniben (Sister Merni).

Tears of joy came to my eyes. I suddenly
realized that I had learned to love these women
deeply and now they were learning to love and
accept me—and to love and accept Jesus.

It was furlough time and as Edna and I
trudged home from one of our last visits to
Vadia she remarked, "It's amazing! No one
has ever had courage to go to that village
because of the dogs."

"God has answered prayer," I responded.

There could be no other explanation. It was
as simple as that. Believing faith had caused
things to happen which were little short of
miraculous—and in the process several dogs
were dead.

Furlough Means...

learning new words which evolved,
adjusting to speed and progress,
listening to problems unsolved,
finding men burdened with stress.

traveling on tour where we're sent,
speaking whenever we're asked,
baring our hearts 'til we're spent,
sharing this God-given task.

longing to find youth who care,
seeing the need is so great!
urging them on to prepare,
knowing that lost men still wait.

meeting the faithful in heart,
thanking them for loving prayer,
counting on them for their part,
sensing our burdens they share.

being with family and friends,
eating good food, gaining weight!
shopping for clothes, odds and ends,
packing and shipping by freight.

looking beyond to our field,
feeling we cannot stay here!
praying for souls who will yield,
weeping for those bound by fear.

saying farewell to this land,
leaving behind those we love,
following God's guiding hand,
seeking His glory above.

—Virginia Jacober

5

Our Wilderness Home

Furlough had been a pleasant change of place and pace, though after only a few days I had been ready to return to India, the land I had learned to love.

We were appointed to work in a new area and live in a village called Radhanpur near the desert of Cutch, south of West Pakistan and 100 miles from the Arabian Sea. We had no idea what this new mission station would be like—a blessing in disguise!—except we knew it would be hot.

After jolting along on the train for nearly four hours, we were sweating profusely. The dust and soot blowing in the windows clung to our skin and clothes. The shaking and bumping gave us both a headache. How relieved we were to finally see the sign announcing the village!

We had been warned to rush from the train if we wanted to grab a seat or even find standing room on the decrepit bus which commuted from the station to the village three miles away. We managed to get on the bus, but our luggage was piled onto an oxcart which took 45 minutes to rumble along the dusty track—the normal rate of speed for those amazing conveyances which can negotiate the most impossible terrain.

From the middle of the village we walked the last half mile to our bungalow on the outskirts. Giggling children called after us, "Budia, budia—white one, white one."

New sounds greeted us: the cawing of big black crows, the screeching of bright green parrots, the meowing and honking of beautiful peacocks, noisy chattering of mynas, babblers and chipmunks, howling and growling of scrawny dogs, melodious ringing of temple bells, rhythmic beating of drums, lively conversations of housewives and farmers.

The smells were varied too: hot spicy food cooking over cow dung or wood fires, rotting animal manure strewn along the paths. The stench of a freshly dug well contrasted sharply with the fragrant scent of jasmine and lemon blossoms.

Our little "home within the wilderness," we soon found out, was still in the process of being remodeled. It had once belonged to a Muslim who used the three rooms as a barn for storing grain and housing buffaloes. Now additional rooms were being built onto each end so that the house would resemble an "L." This would give us a kitchen, dining room, two bedrooms, bath and study.

The narrow, screened porch would be our living room. Windows were still being made, there was no door and the bedroom had only part of a roof. We substituted a gunny sack for the door and whitewashed strips of more sacks formed the ceiling.

There was neither electricity nor running water. I tried to cook potatoes over a little one-burner pressure kerosene stove. Preparing meals in this fashion was time-consuming but adequate, I decided, until we could find a better stove and hire a cook.

Diarrhea usually infected newcomers. Our family was no exception. Danny, 4, and Jimmy, 18 months, both succumbed. Jimmy's condition deteriorated with alarming speed. Ed consulted a village doctor who prescribed a syrup that promptly turned the baby bright red and caused rapid breathing.

Being isolated from medical help, the only alternative was to get him to the Mission hospital down country. It meant a 15-hour trip of 230 miles by three trains. With most of our belongings still unpacked in the middle of the floor, Jimmy and I boarded the train the next morning at nine and arrived at midnight. More bumps and jolts. More sweating. More headaches.

Once at the hospital, a few days of treatment and careful diet brought Jimmy back to normal.

At home in Radhanpur once again we continued unpacking and settling in. We bought a bamboo sofa and matching chairs and covered them with bright drapery material someone had donated at one of the Alliance Women's rallies. With matching rugs and pillows, our little living room/porch was soon cozy and inviting.

During the three months it took the carpenters and painters to finish the house, five different groups of Muslim women, about 50 in all, came to visit.

One of the women was named Zorah, a beautiful woman whose face revealed an aching heart. She lived in Bombay but came frequently to the village to visit her wealthy parents. Zorah's problem was typical of many Muslim women—she had no son. So her husband had divorced her and now she was forced to live with relatives who were insisting that she marry a repulsive cousin. We soon became good friends and she called me "sister."

One day Zorah invited the Bible woman and me to tea. Her parents' home was elaborately decorated with carved wooden cupboards, comfortable swings and beds, and rugs on the floors.

Her mother, a heavy-set woman with a huge dangling gold ring pierced through her nose, welcomed us graciously. As I told the Christmas story and explained the Life of Christ pictures, tears came into the old lady's eyes.

This was a common response among Muslims. Their hearts seemed spiritually famished but a visual acceptance of Christ was usually missing. I cannot report that Zorah and her mother made a confession of faith in Christ. I can only hope that they will be among those Christians who in the resurrection will "rise from Muslim graves."

6

Mena's New Heart

A good cook was hard to find and we were desperate, so we agreed to train the son of a cook who had served us before we went on furlough.

Karshan came and along with him, his wife Mena and their children. He knew absolutely nothing about cooking and we had to start from scratch.

Karshan was a good worker. He waded through fields filled with monsoon floods to go to the bazaar and bring fruit and vegetables and grain. Mena cleaned the sticks and stones from the wheat and then Karshan took it back to the mill to be ground into flour, brought it home again and mixed, kneaded and baked our bread. It was a tedious, time-consuming process.

He also boiled the water brought from the village lake and the milk delivered daily by a farmer who kept buffaloes. For eggs, he went from house to house in the Muslim section of the village. Some of the eggs would be rotten, having lain on a windowsill in the hot sun for several days before they were sold.

Another of his tasks was filling the stove with kerosene. Often it would either go out or flame up in smoke, blackening the pots and pans, the kitchen towels and the walls and ceiling.

Karshan saved me hours of time and energy. There was local visitation to be done, a weekly women's Bible class, Sunday school teaching, a daily first-aid clinic, village evangelism and the literature program which involved editing, adapting and checking books and manuscripts to prepare them for printing.

Karshan became a very good cook. He joined my adult literacy class and although he could not yet read or write he had a keen mind and memorized the recipes I read to him. Usually the finished product was good, especially his pies.

Occasionally, however, there was a disaster. A memorable one was the pudding mix that arrived in a package from home. Karshan prepared it for supper. As I began to eat I bit down on something crunchy.

"Karshan," I called. "Did this box have nuts in it?" He rummaged in the garbage can and picked out the empty box. There were no nuts. I took the crunched bit out of my mouth and examined it. It was a roach!

One morning Karshan came to us at breakfast.

"Sahib, Madam Sahib," he said acknowledging each of us.

"Yes?" we replied.

"I had a dream last night. I was walking in the darkness and something caught hold of me. It said, 'Do you know who I am?'

"I answered, 'Yes, you are an evil spirit.' Then the spirit said, 'Now I have caught you and I am not going to let you go.'

"I was frightened and I cried out, 'Oh Lord, save me.' Then I woke up and I began to pray, 'O Lord, now I know that You are my Savior.'"

Tears came into his eyes as he related the dream.

Mena told us a few days later that when she got up early in the morning she would find Karshan on his knees praying. They also began to have family devotions every evening. When one of the children got sick they prayed for him in the middle of the night and he got better. They were learning about the blessings of the Christian life.

Then came the test.

Karshan's father was a Hindu. Would he permit his son to openly confess through baptism that he was a Christian? A Hindu is not considered a Christian until he or she is baptized and cuts off all ties with his former religion.

Karshan wrote a letter to his father asking his consent. Even though he was married and had a family of his own, it was his duty as a good son to respect his father's wishes.

Karshan waited until the very day of the scheduled baptism. No response had come.

Not wanting to offend his father he declined to
be baptized. Two days later permission from his
father arrived.

Karshan never did take that final step as far
as we know but he openly admitted to having
accepted Christ. One day I overheard him talking with a Hindu who asked him point blank if
he was a believer.

"Yes," Karshan replied. "I am a Christian."

Karshan's wife Mena was uneducated but
good-hearted. I tried to teach her to read and
write Gujarati but it was difficult for her to
concentrate with several children always dis-
tracting her. The Bible woman took Mena under
her wing and began teaching her to pray. She
also began attending the Sunday services and
prayer meetings and showed great interest in
knowing more about Jesus.

The day before Good Friday Ed was away. He
had gone several hundred miles down country
to preach in Easter week meetings. Our two
older children, Ruth and Daniel, were in boarding school in the Himalaya Mountains. Jimmy
and Beth Anne, the fourth edition to our family, were home with me. I had spent much of the
day writing radio scripts, so late in the afternoon I called the two younger children to come
with me for a walk.

Mena and the pastor's wife joined us. We
walked across the dusty field and down the
road with our nine children racing merrily
ahead. While the children played nearby we

sat down on a little bridge to chat.

"On Good Friday," Mena said, "I'm going to fast and pray. I really want to." Mena had learned that this was what Indian Christians do and she wanted to participate.

So early the next morning Mena got up to make bread and tea for her family then came to ask me what she should do while she fasted. I explained that it was a time of meeting Jesus Christ personally through prayer and meditation.

We decided to get together at noon. I noticed that Mena was wearing a monkey god charm around her neck and smiled to myself at the incongruity of fasting and praying to the living God while wearing the charm of an idol. I knew the Lord would speak to her about it at the proper time.

After the church service the pastor's wife took her Bible and went to Mena's house to read and pray with her. It was then, Mena said, that her heart "rose up" and she knew that Jesus had died for her sins! The next time I saw her the monkey god charm was no longer around her neck.

Even Mena's temperament was changed. When life seemed overwhelming and she felt she could not cope, she had often fought with her husband, tearing at his shirt and threatening repeatedly to leave. She had even tried to commit suicide by pouring kerosene on her sari.

Now she no longer erupted into violent volcanoes of anger, pouring fiery curses on her family and resorting to physical violence. Before, she used to take off her sandal and beat her children on the back and the head. No longer. Her very character was transformed. She had become a new creation.

On a sunny New Year's Day our little group of Christians gathered on the banks of the Banas River to witness the first baptismal service in Radhanpur. There were four candidates, all of whom we had discipled: Mena, the pastor's young daughter, our own daughter Ruth, and Babi, the watchman's wife.

That afternoon after the baptismal service, I went out and sat down on Mena's cot in the sunshine. She had bathed and changed her clothes and there was something different about her. Formerly she had worn the type of sari and full skirt which women of her Hindu caste wore. Now she had wrapped her sari like the Christians did and her nose ring was gone.

"Madam Sahib," she said, "now that I am a Christian, I want a new name, one from the Bible." It was a common practice among Indian believers to take a new name when they were baptized.

Silently I prayed for wisdom.

"I think your new name should be Mary," I said finally.

Mena's face shone with joy. Mary it would be!

Over the next few days the awful red betel nut stains on Mary's teeth and lips gradually disappeared.

What a transformation! New dress, new countenance, new name. But best of all, a new heart.

7

Ashes

Late one afternoon smoke from half a dozen cooking fires thickened the air. Gypsies had come to camp in the open field near our bungalow. We could hear dogs snarling, women chattering, children squealing, cattle lowing and men shouting.

At sundown one of the women walked quietly down our dusty path to the well. Her bare feet were calloused, seemingly insensitive to thorns and pebbles that littered the way. She filled her two clay waterpots, balanced them on her head and started back. When she saw us she walked more slowly and then stopped, staring at us as we stared at her. The interest and attraction being mutual, no one was embarrassed.

Her eyes were painted with mascara, her cheeks and arms tattooed. She wore silver rings in her nose and ears, ivory and silver bracelets on her arms, wrists and ankles. Several necklaces and a long tie around her waist were made of brightly colored beads and white cowrie shells. The shells were part of Indian history—the form of currency before the rupee.

The first question one usually asks a stranger is (literally translated), "You where of are?"

The woman's voice was low and husky as she answered, "Kashmir."

After a brief chat she went on, carrying her headload with natural ease and grace.

These gypsies have come a long way, I thought to myself. *They are probably heading southwest, fitting their travels to the seasons.*

They used camels and donkeys, tying to each side of the animal huge cloth bags or strongly woven goat-hair nets filled with shiny brass pots and pans or tiny, black-furred newborn kids.

Field owners paid fat prices for these nomads to camp on their land for the night. Why? So that their herds and flocks would fertilize the ground.

The gypsies appeared wretchedly poor, the children forlorn and naked. But clothing or not, jewelry was plentiful and I was told they were actually extremely wealthy.

The men carried long pointed spears, curved daggers and crude shields. They wore thick beards and a coarse narrow cloth was thrown over their muscular shoulders. They seemed fearless and brave, sleeping in the open at night with only their vicious watchdogs and ancient weapons to protect them against robbers and beasts.

The next day I walked with my children beside the camp and stopped to chat with the women as they squatted beside their fires to cook.

"Come, sit awhile," they called, motioning for us to sit on a burlap sack.

"Don't let your little boy go near that dog," an older woman warned. "It will bite."

The big white dog was sleeping 10 feet away, and I glanced at it cautiously as I began telling the women the reason we were living in this area. They could not read or write, and I wanted to make the story of Jesus as clear and simple as possible so they would remember it as they journeyed on from place to place. I knew that they had probably not heard the story before. They might never hear it again.

I concluded the message with an explanation of the verse, "The blood of Jesus . . . purifies us from all sin" (1 John 1:7).

"Please try to remember these words," I urged as I repeated it over and over.

Do they understand? I wondered somewhat skeptically. Surely their minds were bound and their eyes blinded to the truth about sin and salvation by our enemy Satan. Only the love of Christ could shine through their spiritual darkness. But God could use His Word to bring them eternal life.

A few days later the field where the gypsies had camped lay bare except for a few small mounds of cold, gray-white ashes.

They had come, lived, eaten from the warmth of their crackling fires and then gone. So it

was with their lives: they come into the world,
travel about seeking wealth, and in the end
leave nothing of themselves but a scant pile of
worthless ashes which are scooped up by
mourning relatives and cast into the nearest
river.

I had told them of the One who had
promised to give them "beauty instead of
ashes" (Isaiah 61:3).

8

Angels Watching Over Them

On the edge of the desert of Cutch where we lived ("in the clutch of Cutch," as Ed used to say), there were few wild animals. Occasionally a jackal crossed our path and the Indians told of hyenas which brazenly snatched babies from their hammocks at night.

But in central India some missionaries had shot tigers and in western India there was a government forest preserve inhabited by lions. We had also heard stories of tigers and elephants in the north and up in the Himalayas there were panthers, bears and monkeys.

It was my turn to escort the missionary kids as they returned to school after their Christmas vacation. Woodstock School was located in the Himalayas, a two-and-a-half day trip by two trains then a final 1,000-foot climb by bus. There were 15 children in all, some excited, others weepy at the thought of leaving their homes and going back to school.

In Delhi we had to change trains. I left the older boys to guard the mountain of trunks

and suitcases on the platform where our next
train was to come in. The rest of us went to eat
supper. Then it was our turn to guard the luggage.

Everything went well until it was time for
the train. Over a loudspeaker a muffled
announcement indicated that the number of
track had been changed. This meant we would
have to relocate the luggage of 16 people to the
other track a distance away.

I ran around hunting for help and praying
desperately that we would not miss the train.
What would I do with 15 children, I wondered,
*with no place for them to sleep except in the station
and no reservations for continuing our journey on
the next available train?*

There were no porters in sight so we all
pitched in, racing madly back and forth, mov-
ing the bags from one track to the other.
Finally, just two minutes before the train was to
leave, we got the last of the suitcases and the
children on board. I plopped wearily into my
seat, thanking God for a miracle and secretly
wondering if He had made time stand still for
us as He did for Joshua.

There was still snow on the ground when
we arrived at Fairview, the Mission property
in the mountains. The big bungalow was cold in
spite of burning logs in the fireplace. We could
see our breath in every room. One little boy
even came to dinner wearing gloves.

The cook had come three days earlier to pre-

pare for us. With him for company was a little
dog which he had put in an unlocked room in
his house. A panther had broken in and taken
the dog.

I sympathized with him but he just smiled.

"Never mind," he replied offhandedly, "I
got another dog."

I advised him to make sure his door was
locked securely. And I locked ours.

Late that evening after I tucked all the children into bed and was ready to doze off to
sleep myself, I heard a strange banging noise.
What was it? Where was it? Yes, it was the
metal door of the cook's house.

The panther! I knew immediately that it had
returned for another meal.

As the banging continued, I got up quietly
and double-checked all our doors and windows
to make sure they were securely fastened. The
racket continued until five o'clock in the morning.

At breakfast I told the children what had
happened and they went out to look for evidence.

"Yes," they exclaimed a few moments later,
"there are panther tracks in the snow around
the house."

During the many years our MKs climbed up
and down the mountain, though the woods
between their residence at Fairview and
Woodstock School not once were they harmed.
God had commanded His angels to watch over

them (Psalm 91:11).

><+>-O-<+><

It was Christmas time. We had finally gotten electricity so we decorated our small artificial tree with colored lights attached to a transformer. Glittering ornaments and icicles fascinated three-year-old Beth. She also loved the beautiful packages underneath the tree, including the box with the foreign stamps on it—the one from the Alliance Women's group at our church. It always contained wonderful American treats.

We had baked spicy ginger cookies in a metal oven placed on top of the kerosene stove, and the children had hung their red flannel stockings on the screened porch.

About midnight one night Beth came climbing into bed and snuggled down beside me.

"My tummy hurts," she murmured. I soon realized she was having cramps and suspected dysentery. After a few restless hours and trying what medicine we had with no relief, Ed went to find a doctor in the village. He was soon back with a bottle of medicine. By this time the sun was peeping over the horizon, and Ed and one of our national laymen left for a day of evangelism in the surrounding villages.

Beth's condition deteriorated by the hour. I dug out old diapers and put them on her. I kept running between the washtub, the clothesline and the bedroom, hardly able to keep the supply equal to the demand. Thankfully things dried in the sun in a matter of minutes but I still was forced to tear up old sheets to supplement the diapers.

By noon Beth was lying quietly in bed either sleeping or so dehydrated she was nearly unconscious. She roused occasionally for a drink of water and each time I thanked God for that much response. Dehydration takes place so rapidly in cases of gastroenteritis that it can prove fatal in a matter of hours. I knew this virus was one of India's biggest killers.

I tried desperately to think of a plan for getting Beth to the hospital 200 miles away but there was only one day train from our small railway station. By leaving on an oxcart at nine o'clock in the morning and taking three different trains plus a horse and buggy, we could arrive at the hospital around midnight.

I called the watchman and ordered a cart to be brought.

"Why do you want an oxcart, Madam Sahib?" he asked.

"Beth is seriously ill and I must get her to the hospital," I replied impatiently.

"But look at the time," the watchman replied. "The train is already in the station and it stays only three minutes. It would take the oxcart at least half an hour to go the three miles."

I obviously was not thinking rationally. That solution was out of the question.

But there was a night train. It would be a last resort. I began to pack but deep down inside I

sensed that this too was desperate and perhaps even useless activity.

As Beth's fever intensified so did my prayers.
Babi called the pastor's and cook's wives and
they arrived at my door. One does not knock at
a door—one clears one's throat loudly.

"Madam Sahib, may we come in and pray for
Beth?" they asked.

"Please do," I urged, happy to have some
emotional and spiritual support. We all stood
around the bed and Babi led in a simple prayer.

"Oh, Lord," she pleaded, "perform a miracle
and restore Beth to health." It was obvious
that only a miracle would save this child who
was continuing to get worse by the hour.

Late in the afternoon the men returned from
the villages. Ed took one look at Beth and the
half-packed luggage.

"Where are you going?" he asked quizically.

"I wanted to get her to the hospital," I
replied, the worry and frustration of the day
tainting my voice. "Can't we drive her there?"

There were few village roads down country
and we knew the five rivers would be uncross-
able at this time of the year even with a jeep.

"She will never live until we get her there,"
Ed said, verbalizing the painful truth which
was already breaking my heart.

He decided to drive into our village to find a
doctor. The one who had given us the medicine
that morning was the personal physician of the
Muslim Queen Mother who lived in the palace

which graced about one-third of our village. But he had been called away and was not available.

After prolonged inquiries Ed found a young doctor who agreed to come. He examined Beth.

"The child has gastroenteritis," he said, "but there is a new antibiotic which might help."

We held our breath and waited for him to produce it or prescribe it. He shook his head negatively.

"It isn't available here in the village. Your nearest place would be Ahmedabad."

Ahmedabad! That was two trains and 150 miles away! We might drive it in eight hours, providing we did not get bogged down in one of the five rivers or stuck in the deep sand of oxcart tracks or miss the road which sometimes disappeared between villages, causing us to end up in the middle of a field or come face to face with a six-foot-tall thick cactus hedge fencing someone's property. It was dusk now and we knew such a trip at night was impractical.

Ed left the room. I followed him. He began searching in the cupboard of his office.

"Someone in the States gave me some sample bottles of medicine," he said pulling out a handful of assorted containers.

The young doctor examined them carefully and then pointed to one.

"There it is! That's the one she needs," he said.

My hope soared. Had God—the Omniscient

One who knows what is going to happen ahead of time—had He provided the very medicine we needed months before we needed it?

Indeed He had. It was a miracle!

We began the dosage the doctor prescribed and within 24 hours Beth began to respond. By Christmas Eve she was still weak but sitting up in her nightie savoring the delight of unwrapping the beautiful gifts which could just as easily have lain unopened under the tree.

>-+-◊-·-O-·-◊-+-<

It was 1964 and time for our second furlough. I was on crutches recovering from hip surgery performed in a Mission hospital in the Punjab. The four children and I were going to travel to Bombay after school ended. There we would meet Ed who was packing up things at the station, and together we would board a French ship bound for the Far East.

At the airport I handed my crutches to Ruth and picked up Beth. A mad rush for seats on the plane ensued—no reservations could be made ahead of time. Being slow, I was unable to get five seats together.

Finally settling in, I breathed a sigh and looked down the aisle. Jimmy was looking back at me, his eyes brimming with tears. He had never flown before and I was not beside him for comfort and reassurance. Unable to move, I resorted to prayer for each child committing them into the Lord's care.

The day before our ship was to sail Beth

developed measles. We were advised to bring her aboard anyway and were shown to a tiny room at the stern big enough for only Beth and me. We laid her on the straw mattress which shook with every vibration of the engines. Beth's little body shook with it.

That night about one o'clock, Ed crossed the cold windy deck of the freighter-turned-passenger ship to see how we were getting along. I asked him to call the doctor because Beth's fever was climbing, and I was afraid she might get pneumonia from the cold.

The next morning we were moved to a larger room near the doctor's office amidship, where we were joined by another woman whose baby also had the measles. Within a few hours she and I were both seasick and taking turns visiting the bathroom. Smelly diapers dropped in a pile on the floor added to the nausea.

At the end of 10 days Beth was finally well enough that we could go to our own assigned cabin.

We arrived in Dayton, Ohio, exhausted after nearly six weeks of travel. A huge sign saying, "Welcome home, Jacobers" greeted us at the door of the lovely little house our church had rented and furnished for us. It was a most welcome sight. We could only praise God for His loving care.

One day some weeks later I was home alone (Ed was out of town) when the phone rang. It was Jimmy's teacher at school.

"Your son has just vomited blood all over the cafeteria floor. Would you please come right away? Shall we call an ambulance?"

"Yes," I answered to both questions. I woke up Beth who was having a nap. *How am I going to get there?* I wondered to myself and God. Ed had the car with him. I decided to call a friend. She agreed to come but she was delayed and before we could get out the door the phone rang again. It was the school again wondering where I was.

We arrived just before the ambulance. From there with sirens screaming we raced to the emergency ward of a nearby hospital where Jimmy promptly filled a bowl with more blood.

He tried to explain that he had eaten a lot of Sugar Daddies the night before. Maybe that was the problem. But the doctor suspected ulcers. An eight-year-old with ulcers? I could hardly believe my ears. The doctor went on to say that a surprising number of children suffer from ulcers.

Jimmy was given a blood transfusion and I stayed beside him all night. Someone called the church for prayer and blood was donated to replace what we needed from the bank. The doctor did not recommend surgery but put Jimmy on a strict diet. Within a few weeks he was able to return to school and managed to finish the second grade.

When it came time for us to return to India, some people questioned our wisdom in taking a child who had been through such an experience. Would he be able to adjust to boarding school? Would the problem recur?

"What kind of mother are you to take that child back to India?" one person scolded. "How could you even think of putting him in a boarding school 900 miles from your station?"

Ed and I searched our hearts and decided to trust God's wise and loving care for both ourselves and our children.

>-+-<+>-·-O-·-<+·+-<

While Ed struggled with our baggage and steel barrels, taking them up country to Radhanpur, I took the children to the mountains to get them settled in school. I had no idea who would be in charge of the hostel that year, but God had already provided the perfect couple for our situation. The wife had a medical background and understood our concern for Jimmy's physical and emotional welfare. She was sweet and motherly and said she would keep him in her own home until she felt he was adjusted.

With a sense of relief I climbed into the dandy (a canoe-shaped seat carried by four men) to start the long trip down the mountain and back to our station.

At the last minute, however, Jimmy buried his head in my shoulder and cried, "Don't go, Mommy, don't go!"

I prayed and wept and finally left him in God's hands. It was all I could do.

I'll never forget the day Jimmy's first letter arrived. (MKs were required to write their parents every Sunday.) He sounded content and the matron enclosed a note saying that he was doing well.

The ulcers? They never returned.

During our many years of missionary service, we proved God's faithfulness over and over as we committed each one of our children to the Lord. All we can say is: He commanded His angels to watch over them.

9

Stuck

One January evening we were driving home from the capital city where we had purchased supplies. Before there was a good road up country to our village we traveled by train or bus, and only when absolutely necessary, we drove the 50 miles. Some stretches of the "road" were very rough and there were five bridgeless rivers to cross.

It was dark when we stopped at the bank of the second river. I got out and began to wade across. Just as the water reached my knees my foot slid into a deep hole. Not wanting to risk a repeat performance, I decided it was too far to the other side and too dark anyway to see if the road continued on from there, so I turned back.

Ed and I were beginning to wonder what to do when a bus came along and crossed the river several hundred feet downstream. This was precisely the information we needed—the location of a safe place to cross. We thanked the Lord for showing us the way.

An hour later we were halfway across the dry bed of another large river when we lurched to a halt. The ruts of the track were worn so deeply by oxcarts, buses and trucks that the undercarriage of the car had become high-centered. We got out and began to dig away the sand which was solidly impacted against the gas tank.

Deciding to take a little break from the digging we straightened up. To our amazement and surprise a man was standing beside us.

"Do you need any help, Sahib?" he asked almost shyly.

"Yes," Ed admitted, eyeing the faint impressions we had made in the sand, "we certainly could use some help."

"I have a friend who owns some oxen," the man continued. "Shall I call him to bring them?"

"Yes, please do," Ed responded once again.

The man disappeared. We watched and waited.

It seemed like forever but finally the oxen came plodding into the riverbed. The men hitched them to the front bumper of our Chevy station wagon. The oxen strained so hard trying to pull that they fell to the ground. For two and a half hours with Ed pushing, me driving and the oxen pulling we slowly inched toward the opposite bank. Once there, we thanked the two helpers and proceeded on our way.

At the next river Ed waded out to investigate before we started in. Watching his flashlight bob along I remembered that one of our missionaries had recently killed a panther in this part of the country. It was not a comforting thought.

Some hours later we breathed a sigh of relief as we finally navigated the last of the rivers and reached the half-way station where we would spend the night.

The next morning as we headed homeward two men sitting by the roadside accepted the literature we habitually handed out on our trips. Seldom did we hear of any results from this tract distribution but we wanted to be faithful in planting the seed. God would take care of the harvest.

As we pulled away one of the men called, "Oh, Sahib, I want to come with you." Unfortunately we did not hear him and we drove away. Later that afternoon the man arrived at our door.

He told us that the tract we handed him that morning was the second one he had received from us. And today he was responding to the truth of what he had read. He wanted to be a Christian.

"I worship the Lord Jesus," he stated simply after we talked and prayed. It proved to be a true conversion, for back in his village in front of his own people he publicly confessed his faith in Jesus Christ.

>―┼◆>―O―<◆┼<

Ed and Daniel had driven down country to purchase food supplies. Without warning, on the way home, the car stopped. Ed checked under the hood. It was double trouble. The fan belt had broken and the water hose had sprung a leak. Ed always carried an extra spring—the usual victim of those torturous roads—but he did not have the parts he needed now.

Suddenly out of the darkness loomed a truck lighted like a Christmas tree. It stopped opposite the car and two men climbed out. One was tall and one short, reminding Ed of the cartoon characters Mutt and Jeff.

But these men were not cartoon characters.

They asked what the problem was and when Ed explained, they volunteered to return to a nearby village to see if they could find a fan belt and a water hose.

This was a most unusual offer—two strangers, especially truck drivers willing to take the time and trouble to go on such an errand? It was unheard of! God's angels, we were finding out, did not always have wings and wear white robes.

Ed and Dan waited and hoped. After more than an hour they saw the lights of the truck approaching. The men had found a fan belt but they had not been able to buy a water hose to fit a '49 Chevy.

"What do you have in your car that we could use?" one man asked.

Ed searched. There were baskets of fruit, vegetables, bread, butter and canned goods.

Then he spied the little first-aid box we always carried.

"What's in there?" the other asked.

Ed opened the box to reveal the usual medical supplies. One man spied a roll of bandage the Alliance Women had sent.

"Let me have this," said the tall man thoughtfully as he reached for the roll.

He unwound it and went to his truck. Taking out some grease he smeared it the length of the bandage and then proceeded to wrap the split hose like a doctor would wrap a patient's arm.

The project completed to his satisfaction, Ed thanked the men profusely and offered them 10 rupees for their help.

"No, Sahib," they said. "We don't want your money. In fact, if you need money we will give you some."

Incredible!

Ed and Danny arrived home in the wee hours of the morning. Ed said he could still see in his mind's eye the lights of that truck coming down the road. He believed God had commanded angels in work clothes to care for the needs of a stranded missionary.

10

Vacation with a Difference

Over the years we were in India, many volunteer Christian laymen from churches in the capital city took vacation time from their jobs to come and help us with village evangelism.

These men usually paid their own travel and food expenses and often brought us bread and meat which we gratefully received.

The men would pack our station wagon with sleeping bags, camp cots, food, clothes and Gospels and drive out to distant areas for a week at a time, camping at night under a tree or in the open fields.

When they returned from those forays, their faces were covered with dust but alight with the joy which comes from preaching the gospel to those who have never heard. On one month-long trip the men reached 100 villages and distributed over 3,000 Gospels.

One of the laymen was Manu. Manu was born into a deeply religious Brahmin (high caste) family and was taught to worship idols.

A group of Christians built a church in a housing development on the outskirts of the city of Ahmedabad. About the same time, Manu's father also built a home there and they were thought to be Christians.

However, Manu knew he was a sinner and he began to earnestly seek a way to God. Even after examining 11 different religions he still found no satisfaction, no answer to his question of how to receive forgiveness of sin.

One of Manu's neighbors began to come to his house every morning to teach him about the Bible and sin and how to be born again and receive eternal life. Manu's response was to increase his visits to the temples in his search for peace. But he always left disappointed.

One day Manu picked up a Hindu religious book called the Gita. He read the words of Krishna: "When religion declines and sinful men increase in the world, then I will ascend into the earth to establish religion and destroy the sinners."

Manu remembered the contrasting words of Jesus: "Come to me, all you who are weary and burdened, and I will give you rest" (Matthew 11:28), and "God did not send his Son into the world to condemn the world, but to save the world through him" (John 3:17).

Who would not prefer a savior rather than a destroyer? Manu fell to his knees and with tears confessed his sins and received forgiveness.

One month later he was baptized. His father

and mother would not attend the baptism nor accept his decision. He was unwelcome among his relatives. But Manu determined to follow Jesus Christ and he married a Christian girl.

If you had listened to Air India Radio a few years earlier you might have heard some very fancy drumwork being performed by this young Brahmin. Air India was the only radio network in the country and it was owned by the government. No religious broadcasts were allowed except by special invitation for the Christian celebrations of Christmas and Easter.

Now, instead of playing his drums for Air India Radio, Manu began to play for Christian meetings and conferences and for our own Mission radio programs which were taped and broadcast daily by Trans World Radio.

Manu was one of the laymen who often arrived at our station to join us in village evangelism. What fun it was to sit in a circle and sing Christian songs and hymns while Manu accompanied us on his drums. He was such a Spirit-filled man of prayer that people were attracted to him. Wherever he went, he drew men to Christ like a magnet simply by giving his testimony and facing them with living proof of Christ's ability to forgive sin and bring peace of heart.

Some of our neighbors—both Muslim and Hindu—came to our compound and were converted right there through Manu's ministry. Even two men on the witness team realized they were Christian in name only and wept openly after truly receiving Christ.

➤―◆〉―❍―〈◆―❘―◄

One hindrance after another had been frustrating Ed's desire to reach into the northern area of our district. The enemy obviously did not want his stranglehold on the area challenged.

The hills were sandy and in order to maneuver them, Ed would back the car up and get a running start, racing at an angle over the brow as fast as he could. Sometimes the car would slide back down the hill and he would try again.

Fields also were impossible to cross. An oxcart track followed the railway line but large chunks of earth had been eroded by rains, leaving gashes that made the track resemble a giant washboard.

The river had only a railway bridge and underneath it the water had piled up a deep sandy deposit. These roadblocks were discouraging for the laymen when they had made such a sacrifice to come in the first place.

On the initial trip to this particular area the car had stopped altogether. The men were so weary they flopped down under a tree at the side of the road. Ed lay on some thorns but stayed there, too tired to find another spot.

"God of Abraham, Isaac, and Jacob," they prayed, "You will not fail us. Touch that car and make it go."

He did. And it did.

A year later they attempted the same trip. This time a spring on the car broke and again they had to turn back. They decided the third time to make the journey by train and left early the next day. Less than 24 hours later they came walking the three miles back home from the railway station. One of the men had fallen getting off the second train. His knee was badly twisted, swollen and painful and he could hardly walk. The enemy seemed to be gaining the upper hand.

Once again the team started out by car. They camped out the first night and the next morning Ed forgot to examine his shoes before he put them on. A poisonous insect was lurking in one of them and bit his foot. The bite caused such excruciating pain that he rolled on the ground in agony and the foot was black and blue for days.

Finally one last thrust was planned. Again there were problems. Ed lost his glasses on the train. The guard on the train opposed the distribution of Gospels. The checker demanded the trunks of books be reweighed even though the men showed him a receipt for the extra weight.

But at last they reached the town they had been praying for and working toward for two years. As they approached the outskirts they were met by a group of men. One young man showed interest in the literature and bought a Gospel which he promptly tore into shreds.

Others followed his example.

The situation was fast becoming ugly, so Ed and the laymen grabbed their books and carried on down the road, pushing their literature ahead of them on a handcart. But the clamor only increased, so they turned back to the rented room where they had stored some of the trunks. Even there crowds of people pressed into the courtyard, grabbing and ripping up the Gospels and shouting threateningly.

Finally, one of the laymen was able to slip away and summon the police. Once the police arrived they were able to restore order and gradually the crowd dispersed, leaving the men to catch their breath in the tiny room.

A Christian man who lived in the town heard about the riot and came knocking on the door.

"You remember the young man who tore up the first Gospel?" he asked.

The team nodded in unison.

"Well, he went home and climbed up on the roof of his house to fly a kite. He fell off and died."

The news spread like wildfire through the town. People recognized the hand of God and their attitude toward the Christians reversed. Some of the leaders came to apologize and accept Bibles.

The magistrate of the town also came to personally invite the laymen to return. "And if you men want to lodge a complaint I will prosecute the offenders," he added. The men declined his offer.

By the time the team left, most of the inhabitants of the village had heard the gospel and had invited the men to come back.

The power of the enemy to hinder the spread of the gospel had been defeated and a great victory won—by a kite.

>—+—<>—O—<>—+—<

Living and working with Indian Christians was a unique experience. Their simple faith often produced the signs and wonders which made us aware of God's presence and His care over us.

It was time for a scheduled village campaign to begin when a postcard arrived from Obed, one of our laymen/evangelists.

"I am coming by bus to stay 21 days," the card read. Ed had been ill for several weeks and was still too sick to be away from home. *What good would it do for Obed and the others to come,* we wondered, *if Ed was unable to take them out?*

It was a hot, dusty May morning when Obed arrived. He took one look at Ed and said, "Let's pray for your physical need. 'The prayer of a righteous man is powerful and effective.' "

As Obed prayed Ed was instantly healed. It was a miracle—the beginning of 21 days of miracles. Samuel and Nathan, other laymen, arrived a few days later and soon the team was ready to leave.

As Ed tells it:

Temperatures reached 118 in the shade. Dust storms were so thick that villages just a few hundred feet from the road could not be seen. Nights brought little relief. Food seemed tasteless.

But never mind the discomfort. We had only one burning desire: to reach lost men and women with the gospel.

The terrible hot season was so unbearable that most people sat idle in their houses waiting for the coming of the monsoons. This was a blessing in disguise—it meant they were available, and when the team arrived they crowded around eagerly to listen to what we had to say.

"Why have you come to our village in all this heat?" they asked incredulously. "If you are willing to suffer like this to tell us something, please do."

This particular group of elderly village leaders sat huddled in a thick stone rest house. They were uneducated but they were basically religious and eager to hear the latest news from God. We emphasized the "spotless incarnation" whom they believe will come some day. They did not know that He had already come in the person of the Lord Jesus Christ.

Was it worth going through terrain that resembled the face of the moon to

reach one isolated village of only a few
hundred people?

The answer was reflected in their beaming faces, their hospitable attitude, their
eager reception of our message and
books—and their invitation to return.

Other amazing incidents occurred
daily. One day the water pump broke.
Where in all this desert wilderness could
we possibly find an American part for a
15-year-old Chevy station wagon, we
wondered.

"Don't worry, Sahib," said Samuel
encouragingly. "God has the part somewhere. We will pray."

That evening a mechanic from a nearby village arrived carrying a brand new
water pump!

"Where did you find this?" I inquired,
examining the part carefully.

"In the local kerosene dealer's shop,"
he responded nonchalantly. "Should I
buy it for you, Sahib?"

"Yes, indeed!" I said, hardly able to
believe what I was seeing and hearing.

We found out later that the dealer had
purchased the part 15 years earlier. Just
think—that water pump had been sitting
on a shelf in the middle of India for 15
years waiting to be released by the power
of a simple but believing prayer!

Another day we were lost in the desert

and wandered around wondering which way to go. Then we saw a man sitting under a thorn bush. He directed us to the right path. Where did he come from? Where did he go? On the way back from the village we found the bush, but no man, and the desert was deserted as far as the eye could see.

On the same trip some days later we were far out in the district. The road we were following turned into faint tracks and then disappeared completely in the middle of a field. There was no way of knowing where we were or how to get to the next village.

We looked around for help and finally found a shepherd boy tending his sheep. He was dressed in pantaloons and a short gathered jacket with embroidery and small mirrors sewn in the back yoke. A bright red turban, thick leather shoes and a long bamboo stick completed his outfit.

"Can you tell us where to find the road to the next village?" one of the men asked. "We are lost."

The boy smiled.

"Follow me," he beckoned. "I'll show you." He ran ahead of us, his pantaloons and jacket flying in the wind as we followed him through the fields. At last he stopped and pointed to some thick bushes. The road was on the other side.

*We thanked the lad and began to drive
on. Someone looked back but there was
no sign of the boy. He had simply disappeared! Or was he an angel with a turban?*

➤◄◆►○◄◆►◄

It was several years later and some laymen
were once again coming to help us. This time
Ed developed a fever and slowly began to turn
a dull yellow. The doctor diagnosed his problem
as infectious hepatitis and advised complete
rest for three to six weeks.

Again we were faced with the question: what
should we do? Cancel our plans? The men had
already obtained leave from their work.

"Why not let them come anyway?" someone
argued. "If Sahib must stay in bed, Madam
Sahib can take his place."

Madam Sahib take his place? Me? Drive that
heavy half-ton station wagon over some of the
world's worst roads which at times become no
road at all? Plough through herds of sheep,
goats, camels, buffaloes, cows and bullocks?
Dodge panicky women and frightened children
who dash madly across the highway at any
moment? Maneuver deeply rutted oxcart tracks
with two wheels in the rut and two angled up
on a cactus-lined bank? Dig like a dog to get
out of the sand when the wheels sink in up to
the hubcaps?

I knew how utterly exhausting a day in the
villages could be just from the driving alone,

not considering the scorching sun or the burning wind which seemed belched from a blast furnace. Yet if this was what the Lord wanted me to do He would provide daily strength and wisdom. It would be an opportunity to prove Him adequate for every need and circumstance.

The men arrived. And with them and three of our children I began a four-week odyssey.

One day well into the trip as we approached a side road someone suggested we visit the village to which it led. I innocently began ploughing through a mile of deep sand. Somehow we made it through, this time with no visible angels, but undoubtedly many invisible ones.

I remembered a remark Ed had made once when we had passed that road: "I haven't taken the car out there because it couldn't get through that deep sand." I chuckled as the thought flashed through my mind: "Fools rush in . . ."

Next we headed toward the desert of Cutch. A tiny village perched on a barren rise in the distance. The hearts of the people seemed as parched as the soil they tilled. They drank in our songs and message thirstily and bought our literature. We were thrilled with their response.

Driving on through acres of wasteland, we encountered a number of soft-sand detours deeply rutted from the heavy trucks which carried freight from the seaport to the interior. Past the last patch of rocky road we arrived at a

Muslim village. As we parked in the shade of one of its ancient, crumbling brick walls, a tire promptly went flat.

While one of the men stayed to change it the others walked into the bazaar and held a street meeting. The tire repair had just been completed when the men returned. I knew from the expressions on their faces that something was wrong.

"What happened?" I asked, not sure I really wanted to know.

"The people won't listen. No one spoke to us or bought a book. They ignored us."

We had tried. What else could we do? Despite that bad day, in one week the laymen sold over 50 New Testaments and 500 Gospels. At one large town we had covered only about two-thirds of the bazaar area when our day's supply of hundreds of Gospels and more than a dozen New Testaments was sold out.

At high noon of the final day on the way home we crossed the blazing desert and stopped for rest and food in the paltry shade of a scraggly thorn bush. Our lunch of flat wheat bread and spiced vegetables was always tasty, but the boiled ice water in the thermos was now warm and unpalatable. Heat waves wriggled dizzily upwards and mirages beckoned bewitchingly.

One exhausted layman asked, "Aren't you tired, Madam Sahib?"

"Not really," I replied without hesitating.

The truth was that Madam Sahib had had a wonderful time. God—the faithful God that He is—had poured in His strength to meet the challenge.

He always does.

11

Forgive Us

A friend of ours, a government officer and the village jailer, invited us to accompany him to a fair 30 miles distant. He suggested that we bring along some Gospels to sell while he conferred with local officials.

Bible Literature International had given us a new four-wheel drive Jeep which would make this trip through deep sand a lot less worrisome. It traveled like a camel.

We parked the Jeep under a scraggly tree and joined the sea of people as they arrived at the fair by camel, horseback, oxcart, bus, train and on foot.

Men dressed in colorful clothes with silver button-chains and heavy earrings were playing handmade drums of clay and goatskin which they beat loudly with a stick or the palms of their hands.

The women were wearing their best clothes too: orange, green and pink satin blouses and elaborately embroidered gathered skirts decorated with tiny mirrors. Their husbands' bank accounts flashed in silver and gold ornaments fastened in their hair, through their noses, on their fingers, wrists, neck, ankles and toes. Their rhythmic songs about gods and goddesses were accompanied by chanting and dancing to the incessant beat of the drums.

A merry-go-round and a ferris wheel were set up and cranked by hand. Very few children got a chance to ride because the men crowded three and four to a seat to enjoy this unique experience. Side shows competed in the cacophony with thunderous blaring through a megaphone.

At booths made of gunny-sacks, merchants sold glass and plastic bracelets, toys, cellophane sunglasses, food and fountain pens—one of the current status symbols of a village man, whether he could read and write or not.

Children wandered about sucking chunks of sugar cane chopped from long stalks. They loved the taste of the sweet juice. Danny called them "lollipop trees."

When the men weren't riding the ferris wheel they squatted in groups to discuss marriage contracts for their sons or daughters. Women hunkered in rows gritting their teeth while designs or names or pictures were tattooed on their faces, arms or legs. One man used his boring tool to plunge into a swollen sore. A stream of yellow pus spurted out, some of it landing on my skirt as I passed by.

People swarmed everywhere. Powdery dust swirled into clouds and mixed with the sweat pouring down our bodies. We breathed a prayer for protection against lung infection.

The focal point of the fair was the temple. The ground surrounding it was thick with discarded coconut shells torn from offerings made to the idol. People thronged to see the god, say a brief prayer and offer their gifts of money and food.

Beggars, dressed up as gods, attracted attention to their begging bowls. One young man was wearing a paper tail, thick lips and red trunks, his body covered with chalk to make him look like the monkey god.

At nearly every fair we attended there was one beggar whose appearance was crudely frightening. He blackened his brown skin, fastened two false arms and hands to his shoulders, carried a pitchfork and wore a crown. A huge red tin tongue hung out of his mouth. This made him resemble the goddess Kali with her necklace of the skulls of the 40 husbands she murdered and her blood-dripping tongue. By threatening Kali's curse to those who did not contribute, the beggar stood a better chance of filling his bowl with money.

We began to distribute Gospels, tracts and brightly colored books. The people seemed in the mood to buy. Those who could read were proud of it and wanted to advertise it by owning books which they would be glad to read aloud to any who were illiterate.

Walking slowly between rows of food stalls and trinket sellers we passed a gray-haired man.

He began muttering and that, we knew, meant trouble. He got up and followed us, talking loudly to anyone who would listen.

"These people are propagating religion. Don't buy their books! Don't listen to them!" he shouted.

We walked on quietly but soon a crowd gathered, surrounding us and shouting in unison. We finally caught sight of a policeman.

"Please tell these people to stop following us," I pleaded. "If they do not wish to buy our books that is quite all right. But please tell them to stop harassing us."

The officer raised his stick into the air to frighten the crowd and told them to leave us alone. Then he went on talking to a friend without waiting to see if his warning was heeded. The people fell back briefly but surged forward again, gaining in numbers as others came to see what the commotion was all about. We decided that discretion was the better part of valor and began to retreat toward the Jeep. The people followed.

A large man stepped up to Obed. "Give me some books," he demanded.

"How many do you want?" Obed asked.

"Two rupees' worth," came the reply.

Obed gave him about 30 books.

Immediately the man threw them into the air. His followers grabbed them, tore them up and threw them at us as we walked resolutely to the Jeep. I could feel the chunks hitting my back and thought, *This is for Jesus' sake.*

When we got to the Jeep, our friend the government officer was there. His forehead was painted with white lines—a clear indication that he had been to the temple to make his offering to the idol.

Ed let the Jeep roll down the incline where we had parked it because he had been having trouble getting it started. But as he slowed the vehicle to avoid hitting a tent pitched at the bottom of the hill, the gray-haired man who had started the commotion threw himself on the Jeep, spreading his arms over the width of the windshield.

Ed stopped.

"Accident! Accident!" the man yelled as loudly as he could.

Now we knew what the rabblerouser was trying to do. He hoped to either cause a court case so that we would have to pay him money or stir up the people so they would beat us or set the Jeep on fire with us inside it.

"Oh God, help us," I prayed silently, desperately. If ever we needed divine intervention, it was now.

Ed always had presence of mind in an emergency and this was no exception. He rolled down the window.

"There has been no accident," he said quietly to a large man standing by the window. "This man is not hurt. We have not come here to cause trouble. We are peaceable. Forgive us and let us go."

Forgive us for what? I wondered defensively to myself. We had done nothing wrong.

Was the big man surprised to hear someone say "forgive us," or was he one of God's angels standing there for the express purpose of delivering us from this desperate situation?

The man turned to the crowd. "You heard the Sahib say, 'forgive us.' Now let him go," he ordered.

The people fell back allowing Ed to maneuver the Jeep. It was impossible for him to see what he was doing and the wheels sank into a ditch at the bottom of the incline.

"Oh no! Now what?" I wondered aloud.

The crowd began roaring with demonic-sounding laughter. But before they could close in again Ed shoved the gearshift into 4-wheel drive and we shot out of the ditch. *Thank God for this new vehicle,* I thought. *With our old Chevy we would never have gotten out!*

As we began to drive away the leader of the riot picked up big clods of dirt and threw them through the open windows of the Jeep. Others followed his example and chunk after chunk clobbered us before we could roll up the windows. We headed out of the village as quickly as possible, thankful to escape with our lives.

Our friend, the government official, apologized profusely. "Those people are the ulcers of society," he commented with disgust as he directed us to the safety of the government rest house where he apologized again.

Before lunch Ed asked the blessing: "Father, forgive them, for they know not what they do."

Ed and Ginny, 1943.

The Jacober home in Radhanpur, India.

Ed and Virginia with the new Jeep donated by Bible Literature International.

Ed selling Gospels in an Indian village.

Jacober family, 1962.

Virginia teaching adult literacy to Mena and Babi.

Joseph and Vahali with the homemade
bricks for their chapel.

Vahali's baptismal service at the bottom
of a 30-ft deep well.

Mailman Ranchod.

A layman team with Ed.

Mary at her baptism.

Mena, Babi and Hilda.

A Bedouin camp, Gaza Strip, Israel.

Fellowship in a Bedouin house, Beersheba, Israel.

Ed giving out Gospels to Bedouins.

The Alliance youth group from Jerusalem on camel safari in Sinai Desert.

Group resting while on safari. Missionary Roger Elbel is in Arab dress in the center.

Sitt Alice and Virginia awaiting tea at a Bedouin camp.

Virginia giving Bibles to Egyptian soldiers on the Egypt-Israeli border.

Missionaries Roger Elbel and Louis Zeigler with Arab Christians at a baptismal service at the Jordan River.

Ed and Virginia, Jerusalem, Israel, 1981.

Virginia at a Bedouin camp.

12

The Well

Anew family came to live near our village and we invited them to attend services. Joseph worked for the railway and was from the Christian community. But we were shocked when we met his wife Mary. The end of her nose was cut off and she wore a small patch across it. This meant that sometime in the past her husband had meted out the customary punishment for unfaithfulness.

We welcomed Mary into our women's weekly Bible study and prayer meeting and it was exciting to watch a transformation take place in her life. She was awed with the love and sincerity of Christian fellowship and touched by the practical lessons she learned from the Bible. But when it came time for prayer she remained quiet.

After a few weeks some of our Christian women told Mary that she should take her turn praying.

"Oh, I can't. I don't know what to say," she argued.

"You can learn," they encouraged. "At first we were afraid and we stumbled, but each time it gets easier. You just talk to God from your heart."

With fear and trembling Mary began to pray, first a few words, then short sentences, then whole thoughts and requests. What a thrill it was to see her grow!

One day as we talked together Mary said, "I never heard this before. I know now that Jesus is my Savior. He is the true living God. I lived with a Hindu when I was young. Then I went to live with a Muslim. I didn't know anything about Jesus. Now I have found Him!"

Mary began praying about all sorts of things. One day it was her turn to have the meeting in her home and as we sat on the floor talking she said, "You see my hen with her baby chicks?" They were parading across the room right in front of us.

"Well, that baby chick," she said pointing to one, "was sick and I thought it might die so I prayed and Jesus made it well."

Not long after Mary joined our fellowship, a high-caste woman who had been attending our meetings for the social pleasure they afforded objected to our plan of holding the next Bible study in Mary's home.

"If you are going to Mary's house next week I cannot come. My husband has a reputation to maintain and I cannot be seen going to her house. She is not married to that man she lives with."

I was horrified. As kindly as possible I questioned Mary and found the information true. I pointed out the biblical principles of marriage and explained that she must take steps to correct the situation.

Mena and Babi urged Mary to make a public declaration of her faith by being baptized. She agreed and asked us to set the date. We explained that until she changed her circumstances and officially married the man she was living with we could not baptize her.

One day Mary came to us.

"If you don't baptize me now the responsibility will be on your head." Once more we had to remind her that the condition of her home was the hindrance.

"Oh, it's all right now," she explained happily. "You met my son Abraham the other day, didn't you? He would never have come to visit me if there were any question of my position in the home. We are married."

We accepted her explanation as an answer to prayer. This meant that she was ready to be baptized. Mary found it difficult to wait. She enthusiastically told us about a dream she had one night.

"Two angels came and carried me to heaven. They took me to Jesus' throne. As I stood before Him He looked at me and He looked at the angels. Then He said, 'Take her back. It is not time yet. Let her be baptized first.'"

We smiled when we heard Mary's story and knew it was time to set the date.

New Year's Day dawned clear and cold. Our son Daniel was now 12 and he had asked his father to baptize him. No doubt Danny and Mary would stand with their teeth chattering as they witnessed publicly to their faith in Christ.

The service could not take place at the river because the lack of monsoon rains had left the streambeds dry. The watering trough at the well in our yard, freshly cleaned and cemented the day before, would have to do. The men began filling it with bucketfuls of water pulled up from the well with a rope.

Suddenly they shouted, "The trough is leaking! The trough is leaking!"

"Well, we'll just have to use it anyway," Ed said, undaunted. "It's too late to find another place. People are already gathering around. Keep pouring bucketfuls of water while we have the service."

So Ed led the service as the trough-filling proceeded.

The joy in Mary's face as she gave her testimony was evidence of the new happiness within her heart. Afterward she served tea to everyone as a gesture of thanksgiving to the Lord for this wonderful experience. At last she was loved and accepted not for what she had been but for what she had become in Christ Jesus.

>-+-<>-O-<>-+-<

Joseph was a refugee who had fled across the border from Pakistan during the 1947 partitioning and settled on land allotted by the government.

To our surprise Joseph came to us one day
and identified himself as a Christian. He began
to faithfully attend the services even though
his village was eight miles away.

Joseph asked us to come and meet his friends
who had professed the Christian faith as children in a Roman Catholic institution in
Pakistan. During one of our visits Ed and two
laymen led Joseph to Jesus Christ.

One day Joseph and his wife Vahali told us
they wanted to build a church in their village.
To back up their request they began making
clay bricks by hand and placing them in rows to
dry in the sun before baking them in the fire.

Several months later they invited us to come
and see what they had done. We could hardly
believe our eyes. Hundreds of bricks lay row on
row ready for the new church! Tears filled our
eyes at the dedication, sacrifice and determi-
nation of this newly converted couple.

Joseph showed us a piece of land he wanted
to set aside for the chapel and asked us to
dedicate it. That seemed to spark opposition,
ridicule and threatenings. Unbelievers in the
village could not tolerate the building of a
Christian chapel. Joseph and Vahali, new believers though they were, were learning that the
enemy causes trouble and discouragement when
God's work is progressing.

We urged Joseph to lay the foundation and
put up the walls with the assurance that

Christians in the city churches would help finish off the roof, windows and door.

Then famine struck. Joseph's bullocks died. Food became scarce. The government organized relief work, and by helping to deepen ponds and build roads, Joseph and his neighbors were able to survive the dry summer months. But the church project was on hold.

Then another hindrance arose. The land on which Joseph had planned to build the church was a government grant and could therefore not be used for charity. We spent much time, energy and gasoline driving to various authorities to get the ruling overturned. After filling in long tedious forms we waited for an answer. It never came.

At last, tired of the delay, Joseph built the little chapel on some non-grant land he owned. He and Vahali decorated the cow dung and mud covered brick structure with a picture of Jesus, a cross and flowers. We began holding services.

One afternoon Joseph and Vahali called us to come for a baptismal service. Vahali wanted to take this final public step to declare her faith.

The famine was at its worst. There was no water in the pond and there was no river within miles. As we climbed out of the Jeep I wondered how Ed would conduct this service. Would he take a cup of water and sprinkle her? What else could he do in such circumstances?

But no. Joseph and Vahali had it all arranged.

I could not imagine what they had in mind as Joseph asked us to follow him over dry stubbly fields, up a slight embankment and over a small ridge. Soon we came to the rim of a crude homemade dirt well used for irrigating the surrounding fields. It was about 30 feet deep.

Joseph began climbing down the steep side on tiny steps he had chinked in the hard-packed mud.

"Come, Sahib, follow me," he called to Ed.

Oh no, I thought. *How can Ed possibly do that? His feet are bigger than the steps!* I had visions of him slipping or the earth crumbling and plunging him into the water 30 feet below. However, without hesitating, Ed began climbing down step by careful step.

"Please, may his guardian angel be on duty," I prayed fervently.

Joseph moved cautiously as he waded into the water at the bottom of the well.

"Stay just behind me, Sahib," he ordered. "On this side it is safe but on that side it is very deep."

Now it was Vahali's turn. She pulled her eight yards of gathered skirt around her and climbed down to join the men. The rest of us watched with baited breath from the rim of the well.

It was one of the most unique and blessed ceremonies I ever witnessed. *Did it matter*, I wondered, *where this public confession of faith in Christ was made? In a baptistry in a beautiful church? In a meandering river? In a freshly cleaned watering trough? Or a 30-foot well?*

The meaning, I decided, was not diminished by the location.

13

Plagues and More Plagues

Our existence in India was plagued with assorted creatures which ranged from annoying to deadly and every level in between. But in my teens I decided that since I was going to be a missionary I had better learn to deal with insects and other "creepy-crawlies." Not that I liked the critters—I simply was stubbornly determined not to be afraid of them and to seriously put into action the Prayer of Serenity: "God grant me the serenity to accept the things I cannot change, courage to change the things I can and the wisdom to know the difference."

One day as we drove through the field alongside our house a huge snake crossed our path. We stopped and killed it because we felt it was a potential danger to our compound of a dozen children plus adults. An elderly neighbor vehemently protested our action.

"Why did you kill my snake?" she asked obviously annoyed. "For many years I have fed that snake and kept it in my garden. It has glided over my body while I slept and I've talked to it often. You have destroyed my protection."

We explained that this snake had repeatedly come into our yard endangering the lives of our people. The woman seemed to understand our point of view but went away muttering.

Before dawn one morning I was awakened when Ed turned on the flashlight. He shone it around the ceiling and walls, and the beam picked up a snake's tail hanging down from a crack where the whitewashed gunny-sacks were tacked to the bricks.

As I huddled in bed and prayed, Ed went to call the watchman. Bharna arrived carrying a long bamboo pole with a hook on the end. But by that time the snake had wriggled back up into the ceiling and there was no sign of it. I pointed to the place where it had been and Bharna thrust the pole through the crack and twisted it around.

He caught a loop of the reptile in the hook and pulled it down enough to smash and kill it, its blood splattering onto the papers on my desk. Bharna took the snake outside and built a little bonfire. We followed to see what he planned to do.

"Why are you burning the snake?" we asked as he tossed the snake into the fire.

"Well," Bharna said, "we believe that when you kill a snake it takes a picture of you in its eyes. If you just throw it into the bushes its mate will come to find it, look into its eyes, see who killed it and then come and bite you." Bharna was destroying the evidence!

It seemed ironic that, while we privately battled against invasion from these reptiles, shrines were erected in their honor. One famous temple housed a snake underneath the floor. If a man committed a crime he was taken there and made to put his hand through a hole. If he was bitten he was guilty; if not, he was innocent.

One of the gods is believed to have been born from a snake and is pictured with a huge one twined around his neck. Small vipers encircle his forearms and nest in his hair. His couch and throne are a solid mass of serpents whose heads are raised over him in a canopy of protection.

Krishna, the incarnation of the Hindu preserver-god, is shown posing triumphantly with his feet on the head of a huge snake, its body flung in a wide arc over his head. This is a counterfeit of Genesis 3:15 which indicates that Christ has conquered Satan and eventually will destroy his power forever.

>-+-+>-+-O-+-+>-+-<

Scorpions, some the size of a man's hand, are also worshiped. I was ready to climb into bed one evening when for some reason which God already knew, I took time to throw the covers back. There in the middle of my bed was a scorpion waiting and ready.

Another time I lifted the pillow from our

baby's crib to reach for her pajamas. One lay curled on top of them.

Not once were any of our family members stung. Surely God's angels were protecting us from harm.

➤━┥◆━O━◆┝━◄

One night Ed was away and I cornered a big rat in the bathroom. *When the cat's away the rats will play*, I mused. Not willing to try to deal the death blow I hurriedly closed the door and called the night watchman.

We chased the rat up the wall and when it crouched on the screen I quickly slammed the window shut trapping the rat inbetween. Its tail was hanging out so, while I cautiously swung the window open so he could capture it, the watchman grabbed it and held on. In the mad scramble, however, he was left holding a long tail in his hand and the rat got away!

"There's a puppy dog in my bed," our three-year-old called out one night.

"Oh, darling, you must be dreaming," I answered wearily. "Go back to sleep."

A few moments later she woke us again insisting that the puppy was still in her bed. We got up and shone a flashlight. There in its beam was a huge rat crouching at her feet.

That year, within three months, we caught 24 rats. There was a reason for such an infestation. The Indians set rat traps but they use a cage. When the rat is caught they carry it to the edge of the village and free it. They will not kill life. We happened to live on the outskirts of the village so periodically the rats invaded our compound.

An article appeared in our local newspaper about a unique Hindu temple where 10,000 villagers fed, cared for, prayed to and worshiped thousands of rats. They believed these rats were reincarnations of their family and friends. The rats were proof that their life would go on and that the miracles of their goddess were continuing.

According to legend a Hindu goddess told her followers that after she died she would return as a rat. Barefooted villagers poured into the temple every day, shuffling through a living brown carpet of rodents which converged at vats of water, grain and sweets. If people treated the rats with respect and fed them there would never be a plague of rats on their crops. They had not had a rat plague since then.

But the people had to be careful not to step on a rat, for anyone who accidentally injured one would have to pay a fine in silver or gold. If the rat was killed a golden image of a rat had to be offered to Karni.

The air in the temple was permeated with an overwhelming stench. Worshipers knelt down in front of the altar with their heads touching the ground, the rats licking their hair and fingers. After prayer the villagers left an offering of food or money. The priest estimated that it cost $4,000 a year to feed the rats.

⋗─┼─◆⟩──O──⟨◆─┼─⋖

The first time I visited a home with our senior missionary, Esther King, we were given the best chairs in the house. Pillows on the seat were an added comfort but soon the backs of my thighs and knees felt itchy. I ignored it, not realizing I was supplying dinner for a second family inhabiting the house—a family of bedbugs! I later counted 68 welts that plagued me for days.

⋗─┼─◆⟩──O──⟨◆─┼─⋖

Mosquitoes carrying malaria thrived prolifically at our station. By the time we realized we should be taking preventative pills it was too late. Malaria began attacking me at intervals. I became violently ill with vomiting, a splitting headache, burning eyes and fever.

One attack came when Danny was four months old. I was concerned because it posed a threat to both of us. I had hoped to nurse him for nine months because the example of the Indian women led me to believe this was God's plan for mothers to love and care for their babies. I did not want to resort to powdered milk from a bottle.

After three days and much suffering I asked Ed to call Timothy the Indian pastor to pray. I donned a robe and tottered to the living room where we knelt by the couch. In simple faith the men anointed me with oil according to James 5:14-15 and prayed that God would deliver me. I immediately began to improve and never had malaria again. God's healing work was thorough and permanent.

>·+‹›·O·‹›+·‹

Bats also invaded the space between our roof and ceiling. At night they scrambled on the corrugated tin as they flew in and out, swooping nearly into our hair if we sat outside to cool off, then keeping us awake at bedtime with their noisy squeals.

The only remedy suggested by our Indian friends was to soak a rag with kerosene, light it and smoke the creatures out. It worked.

>·+‹›·O·‹›+·‹

Ants were extremely harassing. The tiny red ones bit ferociously. But most bothersome were the huge black ones which crawled all over our home during the monsoon season. Hordes of them chewed their way through the walls and floors where the poor grade of cement crumbled at a mere touch. They would ransack the house, climbing onto our beds and over our bodies at night, up into the dish cupboard, around the water tanks, under the sink, over the table, even into the refrigerator. We DDT'd them by the thousands.

Our little home also provided many feasts for the destructive variety of white ants. My mother had given me a set of books which I tucked away protectively on a wall shelf. One evening I decided to read a book and went to pull one

out. It seemed stuck so I pulled harder. As I
tugged, the spines of all 12 volumes came off in
my hand. There was nothing but black rot
behind. No books. They were gone.

><><><>

Lizards were new to us. Our first week in
India we found one in our room. It was only
about eight inches long and a light cream color
that matched the walls. Innocently we staged a
wild chase around beds and chairs, over trunks
and under boxes, until we cornered and killed
it. The next morning we described our
encounter to the Kings at breakfast.

"You shouldn't kill lizards," they remon-
strated. "They're your friends. They eat
mosquitoes and moths."

And so we learned to share our living quarters with them—even dresser drawers. They laid
their eggs among my handkerchiefs and sometimes it was hard to tell whether I was dis-
turbing a lizard egg or a moth ball—they were
the same shape and color.

I was going out the kitchen door one day and
as it slammed a lizard fell down my back and
became trapped between my blouse and skirt.
As it began clawing to get out I began dancing
and screaming. Ed and the cook came, both
looking perplexed. They could not see what
was wrong until I loosened my skirt and the
lizard fell to the ground and scrambled away.
Then we all had a good laugh.

Yes, God did grant us the serenity to accept

the things we could not change.

>–I–‹›–O–‹›–I–‹

Water for drinking had to be boiled or treated chemically. Because our well water was only suitable for washing, a servant crossed the fields daily to the railway station to get clean water which he carried back in big brass pots balanced on his head.

A contaminated supply could spread typhoid or guinea worms. We knew about both by experience. Our language teacher was absent for several days. When he returned he explained that he had been troubled by a swelling on the top of his head. The doctor worked for three days removing 28 guinea worms from their nest under his skin. Each worm had to be carefully and slowly wound around an instrument and gently dislodged so as not to be torn, or it would go back into his body and continue to reproduce.

Three of our four children suffered from typhoid with fevers so high they were delirious. The cause? Contaminated water.

>–I–‹›–O–‹›–I–‹

Frogs overtook us in the monsoon season.

I sat on the door step one evening at sunset and counted 21 babies hopping out of a crack between the bricks of the house. Some of them ended up inside the house, where they gravitated to the bathroom to enjoy our daily showers with us. I often herded them like sheep out of our bedroom and back to the bathroom and out the drain.

One night the servant brought a bucket of water for my shower.

"Is this clean" I asked, "not from our well filled with frogs?"

"It is fresh and clean, Madam Sahib," came the reply.

I used the dipper, poured water over myself, soaped and scooped up a second big dipperful to rinse.

The electricity went off while I was showering so I turned on a flashlight to see if I had left enough water for Ed to use.

A crowd of tadpoles was darting around in Ed's bathwater!

><+>·O·<+><

Lice were personal and extremely uncomfortable.

We had been to the river one evening and played in the sand with Ruthy. That night I woke up scratching my head. Thinking I had gotten sand in my hair, I washed it. The next day it still itched. While I was talking with one of our missionary women and at the same time scratching, I felt something catch under my fingernail. There was a tiny squirming insect.

"My de-ah," she exclaimed with her New England accent, "you've got them!"

The process of elimination was time-consuming. A new shampoo followed by a fine-toothed comb netted about 21 of the creatures.

I thought the problem was solved until another missionary told me about nits (eggs) which might hatch hordes of babies, which in turn would mature to reproduce. So like monkeys at the zoo, my friend and I sat from nine p.m. until one a.m. as she went through my hair inch by inch. When the score reached 50 I lost count.

Subsequently, I played "mother monkey" and sat with my children by the hour to relieve their suffering. I could sympathize with other mothers and hundreds of village children whose dirty, matted hair was filled with these vermin. The bites often became infected. One little boy came to me, his head covered with sores. As I began to clean out a badly swollen place with antiseptic, maggots came wriggling out.

Animals also entertained these annoying parasites. We were in a village holding an evangelistic meeting when I innocently stood where some buffaloes had been tethered. Within seconds their lice (ticks) were crawling up my sandals and biting my feet. In the Jeep my feet and ankles began to itch wildly and I suspected stowaways. Several fat ones, bulging with blood, had lodged under the straps of my sandals. My feet were so swollen I could not wear shoes for days.

>-+-+>-O-<+-+-<

Flies carried germs which caused dysentery. It could be so debilitating and dehydrating that within hours a person might not be able to walk or work. Hundreds of children succumbed annually.

Nearly everyone who visits India is initiated with diarrhea. Fortunately I built up an immunity but Ed was frequently plagued by it. He tried every remedy recommended and took handfuls of pills. Nothing helped. On furlough he had no problem, but as soon as we returned to the field it hit him and stayed as long as we did.

>─┼─◆>─○─<◆─┼─≺

One day a slow-moving grayish-black cloud of locusts came our way and gradually settled around us. Their green-black bodies with pinkish undersides inched their way along branches and stalks devouring as they went. Our boys beat drums which scared them up into swirls of quivering wings only to have them land again a few feet away. Neighboring farmers and gardeners pounded brass plates day and night to protect their crops.

Eventually the government established a Locust Protection Center where officers initiated defensive campaigns whenever a siege was forecast.

>─┼─◆>─○─<◆─┼─≺

Terrible dust storms also plagued us. One particular storm plunged us into absolute darkness and was so frightening that some people thought the end of the world had come.

The children and I were outside talking with friends when we looked up to see huge flocks of screeching birds flying ahead of an ominous black cloud. Soon great gusts of wind began blowing. I grabbed the children.

"Into the house, quickly!" I yelled, pulling them toward the door.

The storm hit with such force I could barely push the door shut. Within seconds it was pitch black. The noise sounded like a freight train going over the roof. I tried to calm the crying children and at the same time hunt for the kerosene lamp.

Dust and sand penetrated the closed windows. It was as if someone were sprinkling handfuls of sand onto our papers, tables, beds, cupboards and floors. Our hair and clothes were peppered. Our teeth gritted. Only handkerchiefs over our noses helped us breathe.

After half an hour the storm abated and a deep rosy glow filled the air. Gradually the dust settled and the afternoon sun shone again.

>—+—◊—O—◊—+—◄

For several years we had no electricity. We used old-fashioned Aladdin kerosene lamps. Often we left a room lit only to return and find it dark, with smoke pouring out of the glass chimney and the wick on fire or covered with a thick layer of carbon.

So as you can imagine, it was an exciting day when we got electricity and we celebrated with a "light" Christmas. This luxury had its drawbacks, however. The current was unstable. It fluctuated unexplainably or went off completely. There might be so much voltage shooting through that the light bulb looked as if it would burst. Or there was so little you could not tell if the light was on or off. This was very hard on electrical equipment. We were so pleased to have a new electric refrigerator until it burned out and had to be rewired for use with a regulator.

The unpredictability was hard both on our nerves and our pocketbook. We would settle down to read and the lights would go off. Or we might be in the middle of a bath or typing a letter. We would grope for the box of matches and candles placed conveniently in every room, but by the time we tripped over a chair or bumped into a table or skidded across the bathroom floor, the lights would come on just as we managed to get one match out of four to light up. Flashlights were faster but the batteries were expensive and they deteriorated quickly in the humid air.

Darkness spelled danger because professional thieves took advantage of unlit houses and moonless nights. To ward off prowlers people would leave a small wick to serve as a night light. This provided security especially when they slept outside to take advantage of cool night air during the hot season.

Death, the last plague in the Old Testament, separated unbelievers from those who accepted God's sacrifice of a lamb, and later the Lamb.

We were talking with a group of village women when some men came out of a hut carrying on a stretcher the body of a little girl who had died of tuberculosis. A few moments later women relatives emerged mourning and beating their breasts. It was a heart-breaking sight and my eyes filled with tears as they moaned, "Hai, hai, hai" (woe, woe, woe).

They followed the body a short distance and then turned around and slowly walked back to the house, still beating their breasts. Their sorrow was overwhelming.

I felt their grief. *What hope did they have? What comfort?* I wondered. They had no assurance of ever seeing that little girl again. According to Hinduism no one knew how she might be reborn in her next life. They did not know that Jesus could change their despair into hope, their sadness into gladness.

We were there to give them this glorious message.

14

Count Your Many Burdens?

Sometimes in missionary work it seems that the burdens outweigh the blessings, and it is easy to get under the circumstances instead of rising above them.

A post card from the doctor at the hospital where the children were in school informed us that Beth was hospitalized but diagnosis was uncertain. Mail took seven days. What was wrong? Should I go be with her?

Our oldest daughter, Ruth, had graduated from high school and was adjusting to life in the "foreign country" of America. She had recently been robbed of all her valuables: passport, letters, glasses and wallet containing every penny she had.

A Christian asked to borrow money from us to be used as a bribe. We had to refuse so he retaliated by not attending church.

Violent opposition erupted in our village evangelism.

One of our servants was causing problems.

Evidence of guinea worms was found in our

well water.

Government attitudes toward missionaries were increasingly antagonistic.

A group of fanatical young men visited us and tore up the literature we gave them, threatening to burn our car if we did not leave the country.

It seemed that we staggered up from one blow only to have the next one fall. Our recourse was to cry to the Lord for help. He clearly showed us that we were counting our burdens instead of our blessings. We decided to follow the admonition of the gospel song and count our blessings.

We were where God had placed us and we were supported by the prayers of friends at home. Our health and strength were sufficient for each day and we had been kept by the power of God through two wars with Pakistan.

At one point a government officer had told us to be ready to leave. It was rumored that paratroopers had landed within our area. Pakistan radio even announced that our village had already been captured. Orders were to maintain blackouts nightly so I put carbon paper on the windows. The American Consulate sent directions to pack our suitcases and prepare for evacuation. Wounded Indian soldiers were driven past our home, their bloody bandages evidence of nearby battles. Soldiers on maneuvers camped in the field next to our home and bathed at our well.

A friend warned us that we were under constant surveillance by the secret police because we were foreigners and therefore under suspicion. All of our mail was being opened and read at the post office. However, we continued working unperturbed as God provided wisdom and discretion. We were in His sovereign hand.

Supplies ran low and some ran out—kerosene, cooking oil, sugar. Friends brought extra rations. There was always enough.

A Jeep pulled into our yard. It was loaded with soldiers in full regalia, including camouflaged steel helmets which matched the thorn bushes and bayonets protruding ominously from the sides of the vehicle. Ed was away and the house helpers quickly disappeared. I hurried to lock the screen door before the soldiers came around to the front of the house.

At their call I went to the door. One of them was a colonel who introduced himself by a Christian name. I welcomed them in and over refreshments the colonel explained that he had once been a language teacher for missionaries. He heard that there was a Christian Mission in the area and he wanted an English Bible.

His friend, a lieutenant, was a Hindu. We spoke about Jesus, and at their request I wrote on the flyleaf of the Bible a prayer that would show them how to come to know Christ as their personal Savior.

It was impossible to keep a record of the thousands of Bibles, New Testaments, Gospels and tracts given to us by Bible Literature International. What a blessing it was to have such a generous supply of literature during the nearly 40 years of our distribution ministry.

We went to Cutch for three days of rest beside the Arabian Sea. Friends invited us to dinner and asked us to pray as we sat on the floor with 13 other people to eat. After the meal they invited us to come and start a church.

A Muslim holy man came to inquire about the Lord. He told us Jesus had appeared to him in a dream and said, "Follow me." He prayed for salvation.

A Muslim woman was squatting by the roadside letting the sun warm her stiff bones. We knelt beside her and began to talk. She was 116 years old. She said she had already died once and was taken in the bosom of an angel to the court of God. But God looked at her and said to the angel, "Why have you brought this one? This is the wrong person. Take her back."

"Would Jesus forgive me my great sins?" the old woman asked after I explained His story. I assured her He would.

On an evangelistic trip we got lost. Ed remarked, "I wish we could find a guide."

No sooner had he said that than we rounded the next curve. There by the road were three men. We asked if they knew the way to the highway.

"Don't worry," one of them replied, "I'll sit

in the Jeep with you and show you the way out."

We went through paths enclosed by cactus so high it was like a tunnel. It whacked the windshield and sides of the car as we plowed along the deeply rutted track. But eventually we came out onto the highway! We would never have found our way out on our own. God had answered even our wish.

Count our burdens or count our blessings?

Anna Temple Whitney wrote a poignant poem about burdens.

The Kneeling Camel

The camel, at the close of day
Kneels down upon the sandy plain
To have his burden lifted off
And rest to gain.

My soul, thou, too, go to thy knees
When daylight draweth to a close
And let thy Master lift thy load
And grant repose.

Else how canst thou tomorrow meet
With all tomorrow's work to do
If thou thy burden all the night
Dost carry through?

The camel kneels at break of day
To have his guide replace his load,

Then rises up again to take
The desert road.

So thou shouldest kneel at morning's
   dawn
That God may give thee daily care,
Assured that He no load too great
Will make thee bear.

15

From "Desert Plant" to "A.B. Simpson"

Ranchod, whose name means "desert plant," was born into a Hindu family and grew up in a large village. He became a mailman and he and his family were transferred to our village.

For over a year Ranchod brought our mail each morning. We lived about a half mile outside the village so it was quite a jaunt for him, especially in the hot summer sun or cold winter or the torrential rains of the monsoons. When the water turned our field into a lake and our road into a canal, Ranchod rolled up his pantlegs and waded in.

We began serving Ranchod a cup of coffee or lemonade each day depending on the weather. He appreciated the chance to sit down and rest and be refreshed for a few moments. During our chats we observed that although he had a naturally cheerful disposition he seemed burdened by pressures at home. We regularly prayed with him but his domestic affairs continued to deteriorate.

One Sunday Ranchod came to our service. He seemed interested in the singing and preaching and soon became a regular attender. He told us he had been to the temples and prayed to the gods but his problems had not been solved. He wanted only peace in his heart and in his home. We gave him a New Testament.

One day Ranchod remarked, "So it is by faith we receive forgiveness of sin."

"Yes," we said, encouraged by the insight and understanding God was giving him. It was not long before Ranchod identified himself as a Christian.

"I have faith in the Lord Jesus Christ," he declared one morning. Yes, faith was the key and he had found it!

Because of his work everyone in the village knew Ranchod and his bright testimony impressed many along his mail route. The joy of salvation was evident in every part of his life.

Eventually Ranchod told us that his wife had left him. She had been the cause of his domestic problems. But with his wife gone, he now had the daily care of a preschool son. He screwed a little seat onto the front bar of his bicycle and the boy perched there as Ranchod delivered the mail. That worked all right for a while until he finally persuaded his widowed sister, Kachi, to come and keep house for him.

We felt constrained to pray for Kachi and were pleased when she invited us to hold our weekly women's Bible study on the porch of their home. It was monsoon season and the heat and humidity were oppressive. There were other distractions too: a goat and a chipmunk skittered about the yard, sparrows zoomed over our heads as they dove in and out of the house and a dog slipped through the gate and began munching the goat dung. He was joined by the chipmunk. My stomach churned and I found it difficult to concentrate on what I was saying.

In spite of the interruptions, at the close of the meeting Kachi spoke up.

"I want to learn to pray like the rest of the women do," she begged.

"All right," I said, "all you have to do is talk to God from your heart. Say only a few words at first. The next time a few more. Soon you will be able to pray."

It was not long before Ranchod said he wanted to be baptized. We arranged to have the ceremony on Christmas Day, but the announcement marked the beginning of persecution for Ranchod.

An elder brother came to visit but would not take a drink of water in his home. This was a terrible insult. Then to add injury to insult, before leaving he went to the neighbor's house, had a drink of tea and then insisted that Kachi go with him.

In addition, the owner of Ranchod's rented house told him he had to find another place to live. He did not want a Christian or Christian services being conducted on his property.

A "holy man" also came to see Ranchod and urged him to give up Christ.

A lawyer and a doctor visited him and offered him money if he would go to the temple with them. A fanatical party which was active in both politics and religion threatened to stop the baptism.

Ranchod's answer to all of them was simple and definite. "You gave me no help when I needed it and I was one of you. Now you are offering to bribe me and give me whatever I need! I have found what I need in Christ."

We learned that the young men threatening to disrupt the baptism planned to call helpers from the capital city to come and surround our compound and burn our car in order to stop the baptism.

The Mission's field director advised us to cancel our plans because such antagonism would mean trouble not only for Ranchod but for us as foreigners. It was suggested that we have the ceremony performed privately by an Indian pastor. This seemed logical but it was a difficult decision to make.

Ed visited the postmaster and told him to spread the word that we were not going to have the service, that we were peace-loving people who did not want to cause any trouble. We knew that the opposition would try to arrange evidence against us and make an accusation to the government in order to deport us.

Instead of the planned baptism we had a quiet Christmas service with only a few visitors and no opposition. Ranchod came while he was on his routine mail delivery. A week later he gave a wonderful testimony of the miracles God had done for him.

His little boy developed a fever while he was riding the mail route with his father. Ranchod took him home and prayed. At four o'clock, when it was time for him to return to work, the child awoke from his nap well. God had healed him.

Then Ranchod ran out of money. One day after delivering the mail he was walking through the field feeling very discouraged. He happened to look down, there at his feet lay a rupee note. God had supplied his need.

A few weeks later at the Sunday morning service Ranchod asked to give a testimony. He said the head inspector of the post office had come to inquire about his conversion. It gave Ranchod an opportunity to explain that he had found peace in Jesus Christ. He concluded his testimony with a public request for baptism.

And so we arranged to meet him secretly the next day just before dawn at a place near the village. A Christian layman accompanied us.

From there we drove to the capital city where one of our large churches was located. The pastor questioned Ranchod for nearly two hours to make certain there were no ulterior motives involved. This was a common practice in the

Indian church, because occasionally when someone said he wanted to become a Christian and requested baptism it was discovered that he really wanted a job or an education or a loan of money or a Christian wife.

When the pastor was satisfied that Ranchod's motive was genuine we all went to a nearby lake. Our hearts were thrilled as we witnessed the baptism. In spite of the struggles and persecution Ranchod had endured because of his walk with God, his face shone. He showed us the new name he had chosen for himself and printed in his Bible—A.B. Simpson—the name of the founder of The Christian and Missionary Alliance!

This momentous event, however, did not remain a secret. As soon as we returned to the village Ranchod himself broadcast the news to everyone he met. He proudly displayed his baptismal certificate to the superintendent of post offices and asked that henceforth he be classified in their personnel files as a Christian.

The head postmaster of the state sent a wire to Radhanpur asking how many Christians there were in the post office.

The answer was, "One."

16

Deep Waters

It was 1971 and we were returning from our third furlough anxious to begin our 21st year of missionary work. Some Indian believers met us at the Radhanpur train station and presented us with fragrant flower garlands as a symbol of their welcoming love.

We put our luggage on an oxcart and jogged along through the ruts in a horse and buggy, clutching the sides to keep from being pitched off onto our faces. There had been a lot of rain and the tracks were filled with water. As we approached the middle of the field near our house the buggy driver stopped abruptly. This was obviously the end of the journey as far as he was concerned.

We jumped off, paid him and as dusk descended began pushing aside jungly thorn bushes to get to our little "home within the wilderness."

During the next few days we sought to exchange the mad rush of America for the diminished tempo of the Orient. Roaring planes, jangling telephones and blaring television became braying donkeys, screeching crows, snarling dogs and growling camels. Spires and wires turned into rustling palm fronds and thatched-roof huts. Doves and peacocks paraded across the front yard. The pungent odor of spiced vegetables and baked wheat bread mingled with the delicate fragrance of jasmine blossoms and strong whiffs of cow dung and latrines. These were the sights, sounds and smells of village life in India.

Our kitchen walls were black from kerosene smoke, the gunny-sack ceilings sagged—chewed, stained and spotted by chipmunks and rats and leaks from the rain. The bathroom cupboards and window sills had been eaten away by white ants, and the walls were peeling and beaded with moisture absorbed from the saturated ground.

I scrubbed spiders, worm shells, roach droppings, lizard eggs and mud from the cupboards. Underneath them I dug and scraped out the year's accumulation of rats' nests, mud, spiders and brick dust.

Rats had stuffed paper into the Jeep's water hose and set up living quarters in the engine in spite of its being jacked up in the garage. The four flat tires were only minor complications.

I opened a trunk stored in the garage. It had been flooded. I picked up a plastic bag of rolled bandages. It was filled with water and frogs. There was nothing sterile about the bandages now and I wondered how they could possibly be used.

Just then the pastor's wife came by. She asked if she could have the bag. She took it to the well, unrolled each bandage and washed it. Half of the strips she dyed in bluing and spread out on the bushes to dry. Some weeks later she showed me the finished project—a lovely blue and white striped quilt for her bed.

The old 1951 kerosene refrigerator began to smoke and the soldered parts melted as it burst into flames. The sand Ed threw on the fire to put it out only added to the accumulation of debris of various sorts already in the house.

It was dusk and the electricity was off. We had not yet lit the kerosene lamps when Ed saw what appeared to be a dark rope on the windowsill. He reached for it but quickly drew back his hand. It was a snake—a reminder that we were once again in *the* serpent's territory. We did not know at that moment that within only a few days we would become even more acutely aware of that fact and would need to claim power over all the power of that spiritual enemy.

I began to treat sore eyes and pus boils and dispense dysentery pills to ourselves as well as to the villagers.

We dripped sweat from the heat. Stringing a clothesline in the house to avoid the rain outside only added to the humidity. The wash never really dried and it, along with our moldy shoes and books, always had a musty smell.

We had left Ruth, now 21, behind in the States. The others we had delivered to the boarding school. Dan, 16, was in high school, Jim, 14, in junior high and Beth, 11, in elementary. It was unusually lonely without them after the luxury of having a whole year together during furlough.

On Sunday a reception was planned following the morning service, but it rained from seven o'clock until noon and the fields were flooded. The reception was cancelled.

As the flood inched higher and covered the last step onto our porch we began putting suitcases and equipment up off the floor. Ed was also concerned that the septic tank could back up inside the house. So he rolled up his trousers and strode outside with an umbrella in one hand and a shovel in the other, his shirt clinging to his skin and rain pouring off the end of his nose. I could hear his sneakers squeaking as he shoveled dirt onto the lid of the tank. Seminary had not trained him for this!

In the midst of the rains and the flood the local malaria inspector came wading in to see if we were all right. With him were two other officials. I primed the kerosene pressure stove to make coffee and then found I had no water to wash extra cups. But we were surrounded by water and since this was an emergency I simply leaned out the kitchen door and dipped up a basin full!

Just as we began to consider the flood serious and that we might have to be evacuated, the water began to recede. We sighed with relief as we heard the commotion of farmers across the field cutting a channel through the dirt road to drain away the excess water pouring in from the village lake. Their help came just in the nick of time and we praised God for His loving care.

It had been a stressful few days, more stressful than I knew. That Sunday evening I collapsed. It was sudden and overwhelming. My tongue swelled and my arms and legs refused to function properly. I could hardly speak or breathe. *What was wrong*, I wondered. This was an entirely new experience for me. I felt so strange I decided to just climb into bed.

Ed called in the pastor and his wife to pray. After Babi had massaged my arms and legs for nearly two hours she poured out her heart to the Lord: "Oh, Lord," she cried, "Thou art the living God. Do a miracle for Madam Sahib."

Immediately (yes, immediately) I felt God's touch.

Meanwhile, the watchman had gone to call a doctor from the village. He finally found one who agreed to brave the flood waters which had now risen again from more rain. The two men waded hip deep through the field at 1:30 in the morning. The doctor said he did not mind the water but he was afraid of the snakes who might be lurking there.

His diagnosis was uncertain. (Not until several years later when the same thing happened again did we find out that this was an allergic reaction to antibiotics. I had taken a couple pills which a doctor had given Ed for treating dysentery.)

After a restless night the suffocating symptoms recurred and we were convinced that we should be nearer medical help. The Jeep was not in running order yet so we had an oxcart brought and put a mattress on it. Ed carried me out and laid me on the mattress. I remember plunging through the field, the water swirling around my feet, the road barely discernible.

In the village Ed rented a small car from a Muslim friend who was like a son to us and called us Father and Mother. He agreed to drive us the 160 miles down country to a Mission hospital. Roads and a few bridges had been built by this time but we had gone only a short distance when we came to deep, water-filled dips in the road. It was impossible to go on.

Where could we go? Mr. Mathews, the local government official and a friend of ours, was a South Indian man of simple and tenacious Christian faith. We decided to seek refuge in his home. His wife prepared a bed for me—a great blessing after the mattress on the back of the oxcart. As I lay there I noticed a calendar on the wall. It pictured an oxcart going through a river. How appropriate! Underneath the picture was this verse: "The Lord maketh a path in the mighty waters" (Isaiah 43:16, KJV). God had done precisely that for me.

I was sure I was dying and asked the Lord's forgiveness for past failures as they flashed through my mind. I thought of my four precious children and then said good-bye to Ed.

I must have lost consciousness for some Indian women who had gathered began calling, "Madam Sahib! Madam Sahib!" I roused and began to pray as God inspired me with faith to believe His promise of "power over all the power of the enemy." As I prayed the Lord poured new life into me and I wept with joy as I sensed His presence in the room. I knew He had delivered me from the shadow of death. I would live to glorify and praise Him.

In order not to impose unduly on the Mathews, we sent a telegram to our Mission chairman, Rev. Paul Morris Sr., asking for someone to come and help us.

At midnight he and Jim Evans began the 100-mile trip. Water gushed across low areas and once the engine of their small car died. At another spot they got out and pushed, opening the doors of the car so the force of the wildly surging flood would not sweep it away.

The men arrived in time for breakfast and once we were loaded into the car, drove us back through water that was high enough to swirl past me as I lay on the back seat. At the hospital, with a week of rest and good food, I slowly recovered. By the time we returned to our station the rain had stopped and we waded through a mere foot of water and mud to get to the house.

The extremity of my need, I found out, had been God's opportunity to prove the truth of His Word: "When you pass through the waters, I will be with you; and when you pass through the rivers, they will not sweep over you" (Isaiah 43:2a).

17

Uprooted

We were in our 22nd year of missionary work, and happiness for us was living and working where God had placed us—with our beloved Indians.

For a number of months Ed's health had been deteriorating. I did not realize it until he had a complete breakdown, so our leaving India was both sudden and unexpected. When the final decision came I felt devastated, like I was living in a terrible nightmare which all of a sudden had become reality.

In three days we sorted through the accumulation of 22 years. Sitting cross-legged on the floor I separated our belongings into piles to be thrown away, given to Indian friends or taken home.

I wept. I prayed. I read: "I am with you and will watch over you wherever you go, and I will bring you back to this land. I will not leave you until I have done what I have promised you" (Genesis 28:15).

Back to this land? Back to India? Was God really promising to bring me back to India someday? If it were true, what more could I ask? Right now that seemed like an utter impossibility. The rest of the passage assured me that it was God's plan that for now we "return to the land of our fathers" and back to our "kindred" and that God would be with us.

Ranchod came to deliver the mail. His voice broke as he led us in prayer and then said good-bye. Dinesh, our Muslim "son," brought 100 rupees (about $10) as a farewell gift. It was a reciprocal love that we shared.

As we drove down country I thought back over the years to our intensive work in the villages, to the times I had madly checked manuscripts to meet printing deadlines, to the rough bus rides over village tracks which threw me into the air and back onto the seat with such force that my head ached and my stomach churned.

Along the highway we saw a man measuring his length in the sandy shoulder of the road. He was undoubtedly on his way to a temple and as an act of penance or merit he would lie flat on the ground with his arms outstretched, make a mark in the sand with his fingers, then get up, walk to the mark and lie down again to repeat the process. The newspaper reported a man—*could this have been the one?*—who was measuring his length for 200 miles on his way to a temple to pray for a son.

My heart ached for him and for others we had seen engaging in the pursuit of spiritual perfection through repressing the passions, meditation and mortification of the flesh and senses. To obtain perfect wisdom and purity, they believed that they must be insensible to cold or heat, wind or rain, pain or sickness. This was why one "holy man" had vowed to remain standing for a year. He leaned his arms on a swing attached to a tree and his swollen legs oozed from ulcers.

We had met others lying on beds of thorns, sitting around hot fires in stifling temperatures, lashing themselves with heavy chains, poking a long wooden pin through one cheek and out the other and fastening it in front like a safety pin. Such self-torture, they thought, would give them merit and spiritual restoration.

We had come to tell them of Jesus Christ, who had suffered *for* them to give them salvation and the forgiveness of sin and eternal life. Now we were leaving the people we loved.

When we arrived in Dayton, a friend told me she had been awakened in the night to pray for us. She did not know why but God had put us on her heart. This was precisely at the time we were preparing to leave India. Shivers went up and down my spine as I saw how God, in tender love, was caring for us.

Our children could not understand this untimely uprooting. Dan was ready to begin the last semester of his senior year in high school with friends he had known since kindergarten. Now he was plopped into an American school of several thousand students—all strangers—

and felt no inclination to participate in graduation exercises. I was deeply and painfully aware of his bitter disappointment.

Personally I felt utterly humiliated facing church friends and acquaintances, but they graciously and with true Christian understanding and compassion supplied us with food, clothes and a place to live.

It took months for us to recover from the shock of our sudden departure and the scars healed very slowly. We had left behind nearly everything we owned but we remembered Dr. Snead's warning to us when we left for India in 1951: "Beware of the tyranny of things."

Ed was hospitalized with chest pains but medication for high blood pressure eased his discomfort. A physical exam showed that I was in good health except for a bone problem. When I was 15, I had been hit by a car. Surgery on a knee and hip because of complications had been performed in India but proved unsuccessful. Now it seemed necessary again.

I fought the decision. Who wants an operation? I certainly didn't.

"Lord," I prayed, "haven't I suffered enough? I cannot go through any more. Why is this happening to me?"

This question haunted me until one day I read about Jesus' prayer, "Father . . . take this cup from me" (Mark 14:36a). Ah, yes. This was exactly how I felt. *Let this need for surgery pass. I'd rather be healed miraculously or . . .*

Then I read on: "Yet not what I will, but what you will." I knew I must finish the prayer if I wanted to follow His example and I sensed that He was pointing toward the operation. I finally capitulated but added my own condition with the Lord: "Lord," I prayed, "I will have the surgery only if You will use it some way for Your glory."

Evidently I had prayed a prayer that He wanted to answer, for after the operation I found myself recuperating in a double room. Despite the sight of blood seeping through the plaster cast, I was not feeling sorry for myself, because submission to God's will had brought a sense of delightful peace and rest.

Groggy with sedatives, I picked up the phone as it rang by my bed.

It was Carol, the daughter of the woman in the next bed. She had visited her mother that day and we had chatted together. Now she simply wanted to know how her mother was. I answered as best I knew but it was not long until she began to ask some leading questions.

The Lord alerted me to her spiritual need and we talked from 10 p.m. until one a.m. My mind should not have been functioning after all the medication I had been given, including the sleeping pill I had taken just before the phone rang. But the Holy Spirit took over. As I flipped through the Bible the pages seemed to open at the very passages that would answer her questions.

Finally I asked, "Carol, would you like to pray right now and accept Jesus Christ as your personal Savior?"

"Over the phone?" she responded hesitantly.

"Yes. You don't have to be in church to pray. You can pray anywhere."

That night Carol met Christ. It was a thrilling experience.

The next day she walked through the door with her arms outstretched. We embraced—a spiritual mother and her spiritual daughter.

"God must have brought you all the way from India so that I could find Him!" she exclaimed in her new-found joy.

"Yes, He must have," I agreed, thinking to myself, *If she could only know what a painful path it has been!* But now I understood His design—God *had* been glorified through this experience. He had taken me at my word.

18

Beginning Again

The phone rang in the little home we were renting in Dayton. It was our area secretary from the national office of the Alliance.

"We have appointed you to Arab work in the Middle East—in Israel. Will you accept this appointment?"

Would we! That had been our choice when we first applied for missionary service in 1950. Now, 25 years later, with Ed 56 years old and me 51, we were going to that special land! It seemed too good to be true.

Three of our children had already finished school and were on their own: Ruth was a nurse and married, Dan was in college and Jim had joined the army. Beth was still at home and she would go with us.

We arrived in Jerusalem in 1975 and arranged for Beth to attend the Anglican International School. We would be living in the home of furloughing missionaries and helping in the Arab church in the Old City of Jerusalem.

One of our colleagues asked what we were interested in doing. We explained that the home office had told us to do what we could in English, that we didn't need to learn another language.

"There are Bedouins living in the south and no one has done any missionary work among these nomadic tent dwellers for 40 years," she responded.

I caught my breath.

Bedouins? In the desert? Arabs? Muslims? Was this, could this be the fulfillment of my dream nearly 40 years before when I saw a vision of a dark-skinned man in the desert looking for water and I read the verse: "The poor and needy search for water, but there is none; their tongues are parched with thirst. But I the LORD will answer them; I, the God of Israel, will not forsake them" (Isaiah 41:17)? Was the special love God had placed in my heart for Arabs and Muslims about to be channeled into a ministry much like I had envisioned that day so long ago?

It was almost too good to be true!

"Well," we told our colleague, "we'll be glad to work among the Bedouins. It sounds similar to our village evangelism in India."

"But the Bedouins do not know English," she said. "You would have to learn Arabic."

"All right. We'll study Arabic," we replied enthusiastically but rather naively, not realizing that Arabic is one of the world's most difficult languages.

So three days after we arrived in Israel we

once again began language study. That evening a bomb exploded a few blocks away. We knew we had come to live in the explosive atmosphere between Jew and Arab which had begun with Isaac and Ishmael several thousand years earlier.

We found out that even Arab high school students fail their own language grammar courses. This was not encouraging news for two middle-aged language students! It also was not encouraging to learn that there could be more than 1,000 verb forms!

At one point during the one-and-a-half years it took for us to read, write and communicate in Arabic I wrote a letter to the Alliance Women's group back home and drew a picture of myself up to my nose in water with my hands outstretched, crying, "Help! I'm sinking in a sea of Arabic verbs." Each wave carried the name of a verb form: past, present, imperative, participle, verbal noun, intensive, causative, passive, reflexive, reciprocal, qualitative, doubled, weak, hollow, sound, defective, etc. And practicing the new guttural sounds was much easier if one had a cold and needed to gargle!

Ed suffered a heart attack while we were in language study, so although we wanted (and certainly needed) to spend more time studying, we were advised to get out and do what we could while there was time. And so our Bedouin ministry was launched.

It was an ambitious project. Stretching from

the lush citrus and almond groves of the Gaza
Strip along the Mediterranean Sea, across the
hot sands of the Sinai Desert to the Dead Sea
and the boundary of Jordan were hundreds of
Bedouin camps. Our goal was to reach each
camp with the gospel.

Because we knew it would be unwise to start
out alone we asked Arab Christians in the
Alliance Church in Jerusalem to volunteer to go
with us.

"You don't know the Bedouins," they objected. "Someone has to introduce you."

"They carry knives and they don't hesitate to
use them."

"It's dangerous."

"They won't listen to you."

"They're Muslims—they have their own religion."

We prayed, and in spite of the objections we
knew the Lord had brought us to the Holy
Land for this specific ministry. We were sure He
would provide the help we needed.

And He did. Alice Younan volunteered to go
with us. She had grown up in the Alliance
Church and led the weekly women's Bible
study. She and another faithful Arab Christian,
Abu Ayoub from Beersheba, joined us on the
first trip.

Black goat-hair tents nestled in the hills. At a
large one, Abu Ayoub introduced us to three
brothers—Abraham, Khalid and Mohammed—
who immediately invited us into their father's

tent. The floor was covered with colorful striped rugs and dotted with large, plump pillows. We took our seat.

Mohammed placed a brass pot with a wide, curved spout over the fire in front of us, and when the coffee had boiled, he served it in tiny china demitasse cups. It was thick and strong and bitter, but good. His wife brought peanuts and cookies.

The wife of another brother brought her son whose head was bandaged. He had been hit by a stone. We gave him medicine for the pain and in exchange she offered us some fresh, paper-thin wheat bread which she had just baked over an inverted wok. It was delicious.

The young men told us their car had been stolen.

"Would you like me to pray that you will get it back?" Ed asked.

"Yes," they replied in unison.

Ed prayed in simple faith that God would help them to retrieve their car.

The next time we visited our first question was, "What happened with your car?"

"We got it back!" they responded gratefully. "The police found it beyond Gaza."

This answer to prayer inspired Khalid to request prayer for healing. We pointed out passages in the New Testament where Jesus healed the sick and Khalid read the stories aloud in Arabic.

As I sat there I thought, *An Arab! Searching*

for water in the desert! I've waited nearly 40 years for this! Thank You, Lord!"

19

A Fat Cucumber

Bethlehem was a lovely little town just five miles from Jerusalem. Many of the old houses had domed roofs and thick stone walls just like you see pictured on Christmas cards. Shepherds led their sheep down its narrow streets, and donkeys carried loads of choice fruits and vegetables to market from the surrounding orchards and gardens of Judea.

We had rented an apartment belonging to an Arab Christian family. The back overlooked vast olive groves and the front faced the main road to Hebron. Across the street were the headquarters of the Israeli military governor. He was the person whose permission we had to obtain in order to purchase and drive a vehicle, install a telephone or renew our visas.

Any one of these procedures usually involved hours of waiting in a cold, windy office only to be told to come back on Sunday. This we could not do as it was our busiest day of the week with church services, visitation and special programs. In order to obtain our original Israeli drivers' licenses we made 38 trips to 15 different offices!

The Jerusalem Post newspaper used to carry a cartoon called "Dry Bones" by Kirschen, which portrayed the irony of life in Israel. One of them showed Methuselah being interviewed by a newspaper reporter. When the old man was asked the secret of his long life he replied that he had been waiting for a telephone!

We soon learned what he meant. We waited four years for one! We probably would not have gotten it then except that Ed had already suffered one heart attack, and I was concerned in case we needed to call a doctor quickly. The officials finally responded to my persistence.

><+>+O+<+><

I met Sultani, the wife of a deceased pastor, at a weekly Bible study. After the class was over she took me to her room near the soccer field and showed me her garden of apricot trees, almonds, lemons, pomegranates, figs and grapes. We picked some apricots and ate them. The white, rosy-cheeked ones were famous in that area and very expensive to buy.

Back in the house Sultani washed a large cucumber and put it on a plate on a tiny, rickety table in front of me. She handed me a knife and I cut a small piece off the end. When she saw that I intended to eat only that much she grabbed the knife away from me, split the cucumber in quarters lengthwise and handed it back, insisting that I eat the whole thing.

I could not tell her that cucumbers were the one food which sometimes caused me terrible indigestion. A few days before, I had eaten only one piece in a salad. That night I had walked the floor in extreme pain and could not sleep for hours.

But it would have been unkind to refuse her gift. She had so little and was giving so much. Again, as I had done many times, I prayed silently, "Lord, it's written in Mark, 'if they drink any deadly thing it shall not hurt them.' Let me substitute the word 'eat.' Please help me to get this down. I must."

When I finished the cucumber Sultani brought me another one! I assured her that my husband loved them and asked if I could take it to him. She agreed and added a jar of her homemade apricot jam and a bag of freshly picked apricots besides.

It was dusk by then and I had stayed longer than I intended. Good Arab custom includes not only gracious hospitality and unrivaled generosity, but also demands that the hostess walk part way with the guest who is leaving.

Sultani accompanied me out to the road where I explained that because of the lateness of the hour I planned to take a short cut through the olive groves and the valley up to our apartment on the next mountain.

"You will walk through there without your husband?" Sultani asked.

"Yes," I replied. "The Lord is with me."

"Ma Salaami (Go in peace)," she said.

"God protect you," I responded.

I started down the path, a twinge of apprehension passing through my mind as I approached the grove. I had heard stories of women who unwisely walked alone at night and were attacked or stabbed or even murdered. Though these incidents were rare I had no desire to become a target for someone who might be out looking for such an opportunity. Anyone could be lurking among those gnarled and twisted trees that loomed like grotesque monsters in the night shadows.

The light was fading and the darker it grew the faster I walked, tense and alert to the night sounds of owls and bats and rodents.

The narrow path was all stones as were the low walls on each side. Through my mind flashed Psalm 91:11-12: "For he will command his angels concerning you to guard you in all your ways; they will lift you up in their hands, so that you will not strike your foot against a stone." I felt comforted and protected as I negotiated the rough path that seemed to stretch endlessly into the darkness.

Remembering the cucumber, I vowed as I trudged along that if God did not miraculously deliver me from a bad case of indigestion, I would learn to endure it with longsuffering for Jesus' sake. I had been trying to memorize the Arabic word for longsuffering. In fact, I was working on committing to memory all the Arabic words for the nine fruits of the Spirit. *This is a good opportunity to put them into prac-*

tice, I mused.

At last I left the olive grove behind and began climbing the mountain toward the main road. The path widened and a car descended, the beams of its bright headlights picking me out as I stepped to one side to let it pass.

"Oh Lord," I cried silently, "take care of me."

The car slowed but then went on.

I ran nearly the rest of the way and uttered a sigh of relief as I reached the big stone houses of our neighborhood and scurried up the stairs to our apartment.

"Thank You, Lord," I whispered as I turned the key in the door. "Thank You for bringing me home safely."

And the cucumber?

That night I had not even the slightest twinge of indigestion!

20

Mount Sinai

Suitcases, sleeping bags, a small primus cookstove, food, water, Bibles, New Testaments, books, tracts and ourselves—all were packed into the VW Dasher station wagon for our first trip to the Sinai Peninsula.

Along the road winding around the Judean hills south of Bethlehem, donkeys carried bundles of sheaves and loads of kids of both kinds. One poor donkey supported an adult plus eight children—three perched on steel frames fastened on each side, one in front of the mother and one behind.

We passed soldiers patrolling the West Bank and the remains of a bombed bus shelter. Fields of onions and wheat were being harvested. Vineyards and olive groves dotted the hillsides. Ancient landmarks—piles of stones—delineated property lines.

Shepherds led their flocks. One young boy, like David, played his flute as he guarded his sheep. An older man smiled as he accepted the New Testament we offered. One lamb strayed too far so the shepherd put a stone in his sling and threw it so that it landed precisely in front of the lamb's nose. The startled lamb immediately returned to the shepherd.

A Bedouin tent and a camel stood silhouetted against the sky. A woman wearing a purple-embroidered dress, scarlet belt and black scarf watered flocks at an ancient well. Deep grooves had been etched in the stones of the rim by ropes used to pull up the water.

Along the Dead Sea a vast residue of salt formations—like giant toadstools as big as chairs—glittered in the blazing sun. Farther south near Sodom the land lay desolate, barren, stony—God's punishment for the wickedness of the people who had disregarded His rules of morality. Sand and wind had eroded caves and crevasses in the limestone. Sparse bushes interspersed with an occasional thorny acacia tree.

The heat was stifling.

We showed our passports at the army checkpost. A road sign warned, "Danger when bridge flooded." Another read, "Danger—area mined." Farther along three signs placed at intervals caught our attention.

"Danger—firing on the right."

"Danger—firing on the left."

"Danger—firing on both sides."

The IDF—Israeli Defense Force—practiced frequently with armored vehicles and artillery in this area. We could not safely leave the car.

Beyond the wilderness of Paran, where the children of Israel walked with Moses, were sandy mountains strewn with brown stones.

They looked like scoops of vanilla ice cream dripping with chocolate topping! An occasional cloud broke the heat of the sun, and we could understand why God had sent a cloud by day to protect His people in this furnace-like wilderness.

Farther along, Jewish kibbutzim (community farms) and citrus groves replaced tumbleweed and barren land. The desert was blossoming like a rose, fulfilling God's promise.

After a lunch break under a palm tree at an oasis we sped past a nature reserve for deer, oryx, emu and wild donkeys. Solomon's Pillars and mines from which the famous turquoise Elat stone is taken were just off the highway. Soon the lovely Red Sea appeared with freighters, yachts and glass-bottomed boats anchored in the harbor. Hundreds of imported Japanese cars were sandwiched into huge storage lots.

"Show your identification," ordered a soldier at one of the three checkpoints we would have to maneuver on this trip. We pulled out our passports.

"Why are you driving a car with West Bank license plates?" the guard asked.

"I am a minister in the church," Ed explained.

The soldier wrote down our license number and went inside a little hut to telephone the information to army headquarters. We waited. He finally returned and, with clearance con-

firmed, handed us our passports and waved
us on.

The water of the Red Sea glimmered in
turquoise, blue and purple from the colorful sea
urchins, coral and tropical fish living underneath the surface. Acres of pink and blue stones
filled the valleys. Camels nibbled at acacia trees
and Bedouin women spun yarn from the wool
of their sheep as they watched over them.

I was looking at the vast expanse of sand
and stones in the distance when I suddenly
saw a man slowly trudging across the desert. A
lump rose in my throat. The scene was an exact
replica of the vision I had seen 40 years before
when I was reading Isaiah 41:17, "The poor
and needy search for water, but there is none;
their tongues are parched with thirst. But I the
LORD will answer them; I, the God of Israel, will
not forsake them." That vision was now being
fulfilled before my very eyes, confirming our
belief that we were precisely where God wanted
us to be, doing what He wanted us to do.

At a fishing village beside the sea we offered
a Bible to a young man sitting with friends on a
mat in the sun. He accepted the book and as
he began to read it he looked at us and said,
"Thank you very much. This is just what I've
been wanting for a long time. I'm so glad to
have it. Thank you."

"Do you know what it is?" I asked, somewhat
surprised by his openness and candor. "It's the
Bible, God's Word."

"Yes, I understand," he responded. "I have been wanting to read it. Thank you."

At last we arrived at the foot of Mount Sinai. It was after midnight by the time we replenished our gas tank and ourselves and settled down to sleep in the car.

I was just dozing off when a busload of Israeli tourists arrived and prepared to climb the mountain. Taking advantage of the occasion, I grabbed a handful of dates and apricots, the water canteen, my Bible, flashlight and hat and joined the crowd. It was almost two a.m.

The Israelis climbed like mountain goats and I was soon left far behind. *Should I go on alone?* I wondered. I sat on a stone to rest and to ponder the answer to my question. I turned on the flashlight and my Bible fell open to Joshua 1:5-6: "As I was with Moses, so I will be with you; I will never leave you nor forsake you. Be strong and courageous . . ." That was my answer.

I got up off the rock and resumed the trek. A couple of hours later I heard voices. It was the tour group going down!

Another several hours later I reached the small, flat area at the top of the mountain. The journey had taken about six hours in all. Exhausted, I sat down and wondered how I would ever be able to negotiate the downward trail. I snacked on dried fruit and sipped water, thankful for the privilege of communing with the Lord at the very spot where Moses did.

Then I prayed for divine help to begin the downward journey. I did not want to damage my artificial hip joint.

The answer came clear and with power: "He will command his angels concerning you to guard you carefully; they will lift you up in their hands, so that you will not strike your foot against a stone."

Some hours later I walked past the monastery and out into the parking lot, relieved to be back safely. Ed had been wondering what had happened to me.

I soon learned that I was not the only one the angels were caring for. Ed told me that while I was at the top of the mountain praying for him some young Jewish men pushed their way into the car as he sat reading.

"Bethlehem, Bethlehem!" they shouted. They had seen the car's West Bank license plates and had assumed Ed was an Arab.

He managed to push them out, then locked the door and drove for help to a bus driver he had been talking with earlier. The man reprimanded the intruders and explained to Ed that they were on a tour from a reformatory. They no doubt intended to rob him or steal the car.

A few days later we headed for home. We had visited some Bedouin tents, yet many others remained to be reached. Would we ever be able to get to them all?

Time was running out faster than we knew.

21

The Good Samaritan

It was dusk when our visiting friends skidded back down the Serpentine Path on the mountain of Masada where the Jews made their last stand against the Romans. We climbed into our station wagon and started along the Dead Sea toward Jericho, one of the most picturesque drives in all of Israel.

The night grew dark—actually pitch black—and the silence made us feel like we were the only people in the world. Then suddenly the quiet was shattered by two shots. I thought Israeli soldiers were shooting at us because this was a border road between Israel and Jordan and sometimes a curfew was imposed.

Ed stopped the car, got out and looked around. No soldiers were to be seen. But we had two flat tires! The "shots" we heard were our tires blowing out. A flashlight revealed that we had hit the sharp edge of the eroded blacktop and had bent the rims of both wheels.

Ed and our friend changed the one tire. But who carries two spare tires? We certainly did not. So there we sat. Both men tried using a rock to pound out the bent rim, but all to no avail. It was clear there was nothing to do but wait for help to arrive—sometime.

Suddenly out of the darkness a tractor appeared. The tailgate of the station wagon was up as the driver approached so he could not see our license plate. Because we were living in Bethlehem in the West Bank we had blue Arab license plates. We called them our "blue plate special." A Hebrew letter beside each plate signified the town of residence. Israelis had yellow plates. In this way the army and police knew exactly where everyone was from.

The tractor passed us. Then the driver swung it around and shone his light on our front plate. *When he finds out we are from Arab territory he will go on,* I thought dismally to myself. But to my surprise he stopped the tractor and got off.

"What is the problem?" he inquired kindly.

Ed explained what had happened, then added, "We need a heavy hammer to pound out the rim of this wheel."

The stranger disappeared and moments later returned with a hammer. Within 10 minutes he had pounded out the rim.

"Now put on the tire," he ordered.

They did.

"Now pump air into it."

They did.

"Now put it on the car."

"Oh, wait a minute," exclaimed our young guest. "I'm a metallurgist. I know that rim cannot possibly be pounded smooth enough to hold air in that tire."

To prove his point he took our water jug and poured some over the tire. Tiny bubbles appeared. The stranger gave it one more wham with the hammer and the men put the tire on the car.

Thanking the Good Samaritan profusely Ed asked, "Are you from around here?"

"No, I'm just here to help you," came the unusual reply. The stranger climbed onto his tractor, we got into our car and we both headed down the road in the same direction. But that was the last we saw of the man or the tractor even though we should obviously have passed him on the road.

As we drove on, our metallurgist friend said, "We'll have to stop every 10 or 15 minutes and pump air into that tire. It cannot possibly hold." With 50 or 60 miles yet to go, that was not a happy prospect.

But we did not have to stop once! We arrived home several hours later, the tire still holding.

The next morning Ed drove to a garage and took out the flat tire.

"Can you repair this?" he asked the attendant.

"Well, I'll try," he said, looking skeptically at the damaged rim. It took him three hours to do what the "angel" had done in 10 minutes.

Then Ed had a thought. "Would you mind taking off this other wheel to see if it needs balancing?" Ed asked, pointing to the one the "angel" had repaired.

The man put it on his machine.

"It's all right," he observed casually. "It doesn't need anything."

God's Good Samaritan had done his job—perfectly!

22

The Spice of Variety

The sky was a clear, cloudless blue as we drove south into the desert. A cool breeze was blowing rather than the hot, whining wind that usually swept across this vast wasteland.

A few brave poppies, yellow and white daises and pretty purple wildflowers blossomed in scattered patches. But even they petered out as we penetrated Sinai's barrenness.

Camels grazing on prickly bushes were barely discernible against huge, rippled sand dunes. Others plodded up the ridges and stood silhouetted momentarily against the sky.

Then, not far from the road, we saw what we had been looking for—Bedouin tents. At intervals along the way we had seen rusty signs saying, "Danger—this area contains mines. Do not leave the road." But since the area around the tents was unmarked we drove as close as we could and parked the car.

A watchdog began barking as we came near. A young woman went to tie him up.

"He is vicious," she explained. "He has even bitten me. Come this way," she said as she motioned us in a wide circle around him.

We noticed that another tent was ready to be pitched near hers and assumed the tribe had recently moved here since we did not remember seeing them on previous trips.

"Salaam aleikum (peace to you)," we greeted the family.

"Wa aleikum salaam (and to you, peace)," they responded.

Stooping to enter the tent, we noticed that the woman's clothes were ragged and odds and ends of old cans and wood lay scattered here and there. Gunny sacks covered the floor of the tent. No beautiful carpets or plump pillows here.

The woman kept wrapping her black head scarf around her neck and across her face in a modest attempt to keep her mouth covered. Her voice was muffled but her lovely eyes smiled as she chatted with us. Children clung to her skirts, their fat cheeks and happy faces reflecting her loving care.

With bits of branches and tumbleweed the woman patiently started a fire in the middle of the earthen floor. It was soon crackling under a blackened pot of water and powdered tea. While we waited for the water to boil I showed her the Wordless Book.

"You cannot take a sinful heart to heaven to live with God," I explained pointing to the black page.

"No, it must be white!" she responded

unhesitatingly.

The next page was the red one representing Jesus' death on the cross and I told her how His blood cleanses from sin.

When I turned to the white page her eyes sparkled. "There it is! The white heart!" she exclaimed.

Her comprehension of the simple gospel truth amazed and thrilled us. God's Word was falling on fertile soil. We gave her a Bible and other literature which she promptly wrapped in a cloth and tucked away in an old wooden box.

Pouring two big handfuls of sugar into the tea, she picked up a stick from the ground, dusted it off with her fingers and stirred briskly. We drank from borrowed glasses brought by her neighbor. The sweet tea was welcome and refreshing. And Ed, a borderline diabetic, never felt any side-effects.

Perhaps I will never see this new friend again, I mused with some prophetic accuracy (her region of the Sinai was later returned to Egyptian control). But our hearts had been won by this gentle Bedouin woman.

We shared a few gifts with the family in return for their hospitality and as we left I prayed: "May her tent—and her heart—become Christ's dwelling place."

>-+-<>-O-<>-+-<

The 15 Bedouin tribes living in southern Israel and the Sinai Peninsula preserve ancient biblical culture and customs to this day.

They trace their origin to the nomads of Arabia who migrated to the region several hundred years ago. The land is divided into tribal areas each with water and pasture for their flocks. The livestock are moved along with the family from one grazing area to another according to the seasons.

A sheik is an elected tribal chief who manages its affairs. Appointed judges sit in court to decide issues based on laws similar to those God gave to Moses.

Bedouin food, clothing and shelter are nearly identical to that of Abraham. The men plough with camels and harvest by hand, often with a scythe. Those who live along the peninsula's seacoast are fishermen. Many younger men work for the Israelis.

Bedouin men buy and sell livestock, market their produce and fight to protect their possessions and family honor. The price of a bride, who is often a cousin of the husband-to-be, is usually seven camels.

Bedouin women are responsible for tending the flocks, cooking the food and managing the family and home. Their tent is made by weaving goat and camel hair and it can be folded and carried when the family moves. In summer, dwellings are made of desert bushes which allow natural air-conditioning.

The women wear long dresses to protect themselves from the hot sun and blowing sand. The dress is embroidered with colorful threads in various designs and patterns. The veil which hides the woman's face from strangers is made of coins and beads.

Bedouins fear God and pray sincerely. Some visit the tombs of holy men or ancestors, taking goats as an offering. The village holy man may mediate with God on behalf of its families or animals, and Bedouins pray earnestly for God's protection from natural disasters and wild animals: "O Allah, protect me from the scorpion's tail, the mustachioed centipede, the sidewinder viper, slithering black cobra and the spider, 'mother of graves.' "

As a good-luck charm the Bedouins sometimes smear the sacrificial blood of a sheep or goat on a camel's neck.

Bedouins are extremely warmhearted, gracious, friendly and generous people. Our custom was to drive as close to their tents as we could, then get out and walk, praying that the Lord would protect us from the vicious dogs whose ears were cut off when they were puppies so they would be better watchdogs. They often came toward us with their teeth bared, barking furiously. I learned that picking up a stone and pretending to throw it caused the dogs to tuck their tails between their legs and slink away. On other occasions only God's angels kept us from serious harm.

>⤙⤕⭘⤙⤕⤚

One day we were welcomed by an elderly man named Abu Abraham (Father of Abraham, the oldest son) who invited us to take a seat on the rugs in his crowded goat-hair, gunny-sack patched tent. The flaps were up on both sides to let a breeze flow through.

Leaning on the ever-present pillows, we introduced ourselves and explained that our four children were grown and we were alone. Families are of primary importance to a Bedouin and because most of them are Muslims they are permitted to have up to four wives if they can support them. This means there might be any number of children living in a separate tent or room with their mother. Multiply eight or 10 children by each wife and it becomes a sizable tribe!

"Is this your wife?" asked our host nodding in my direction.

"Yes," replied my husband.

The man eyed my gray hair.

"Well, why don't you get a younger one?"

His logic was understandable. Muslim custom permits a man to take a younger wife as soon as the older one can no longer have children. Israeli radio reported that a sheik who died near Beersheba left 51 wives (four at a time are permitted, but divorce is easy) and more than 300 children!

A number of children ranging in age from two to 10 gathered to listen as I explained the colors of the Wordless Book. One of the older boys began reading the tract I gave him and each of the children begged for a Gospel. They had learned to read at the village school.

We prepared to leave but Abu Abraham urged us to stay and eat bread. So while we talked and waited for the bread to bake we watched a young chicken wage a pecking war with a lame dove huddled beside a box in a dark corner. Other chicks of all sizes roamed here and there along with a cat and some small goats. A newborn kid curled up into a furry ball in my lap and promptly fell asleep.

Our teenager brought yogurt made from sheep milk and poured it from a goatskin into a bowl. Then she brought white butter and finally the fresh-baked wheat bread. We tore off small bite-sized pieces of bread and dipped them into the bowl of yogurt. Remembering that it is rude as well as unsanitary to bite from a piece of bread and then dip it in again when one central dish is used by everyone we were careful not to offend anyone.

While we ate, a sudden gust of wind swept through the tent bringing with it a sprinkling of sand which settled like pepper on the bowl of yogurt. Abu Abraham noticed the dirt, picked up a spoon, skimmed off the dust and tossed it on the ground beside his feet. We ignored the interruption and continued eating.

Then, without warning, a chicken decided to cross from one side of the tent to the other and flapping and squawking dashed through our plates of food. Again we went on eating and smiled understandingly as our hosts chased the chickens out and pulled down the sides of the tent.

At another tent we were welcomed by two young men and their gray-haired mother. Her hair was arranged in fancy braids fastened with colored bobby pins. Her friendly face was covered with tatoo marks.

While she made tea, one of the sons revealed that his relatives several miles away had told him about us. He listened intently as we shared the gospel story and seemed to sympathize with what we said.

But it was his insightful comment that both saddened and challenged us: "It's not enough for you," he said, "to give us the books and an explanation. You need to sit down with us and teach us daily, like in a school, so we can ask questions. Then you can explain and we can understand."

Yes, yes, our hearts silently cried out in response to this young man's plea. But someone else would have to do that. Our time was almost gone.

23

Going Home

It was furlough time 1984. Ed had turned 65 on our 37th wedding anniversary—June 21. We spent a long and happy day in the desert of North Sinai visiting Bedouins. We had made many friends among them, had shared their food and fellowship, their joys and sorrows. Now it was time to leave, but not forever, because the Mission had asked us to return. We were delighted at the prospect.

The Lord provided a home and car for us in Dayton and as soon as we could we headed south to visit Beth and her husband in Mississippi and Dan in Atlanta. It was wonderful to see our children again.

Back home in Dayton, Ed remarked to Jean, my Nyack classmate, "I'm living on borrowed time." I knew he was right. His first heart attack had occurred when we were studying Arabic in 1977, brought on no doubt by weight gain, high blood pressure and the stress of learning a new language. The doctor at the Jerusalem hospital had recommended surgery, but Ed decided to try the alternative—rest and medication.

This worked well until five years later when Ed noticed that his blood pressure had risen considerably. The doctor was unavailable so Ed doubled his medicine. The next morning his pulse was 44—at least 30 points below normal. By the time the skeleton sabbath staff at the hospital got around to examining him it was down to 35. Emergency surgery was performed to install a temporary pacemaker but during the procedure Ed's heart stopped. I saw a nurse racing down the hall and I cried out, "Lord, it's not time for him to go yet!" Apparently God agreed, for we were able to finish our complete term.

Now home on furlough, Ed had lost both weight and strength, and as we prepared to go to Nyack for furlough seminar (the pre-missionary tour training session for furloughing missionaries) even to carry a suitcase was more than he could handle.

The seminar was stimulating and spiritually refreshing and we looked forward to the farewell banquet. After dinner we returned to Simpson Hall. Ed suggested we sit in the lounge for a few minutes before making our way upstairs. We found an empty sofa, and he struck up a conversation with a student while I perused *The Missionarian*, the Nyack yearbook.

Suddenly there was dead silence. I glanced toward Ed. He was leaning back on the sofa, his eyes closed.

"No, don't do this," I cried.

But I knew he was gone. I pulled him down on the sofa, asked the student to take his shoes off and shouted to the girl at the reception desk to call an ambulance. Then I began artificial respiration.

Within minutes some of our medical missionaries appeared. I stood quietly aside as they took over. The unknown student came and stood beside me and put his arm around my shoulders. I was touched and comforted by his loving gesture.

Paramedics arrived but could get no response. I joined them in the ambulance as they whisked Ed, sirens screaming, to Nyack hospital.

Rev. Robert Reed, our area director, sat in the waiting room with me until the doctor confirmed that Ed was gone. Then he took me back to the college and Harriette Stebbins Irwin, a cherished Nyack classmate, came to stay with me.

I climbed onto the upper bunk and sat cross-legged as the tears began to flow. Dan called and we cried together over the phone. The remainder of that dark night I spent weeping in the solitude.

The next morning I went to select a casket and Esther King, the wife of Louis L. King, president of the Alliance and former co-worker in India, drove me to their home to await my friend Jean's arrival from Dayton.

That night a beautiful full moon rose, sprinkling a shining path across the Hudson River.

Back at Simpson Hall, Jean and I knelt at the dorm room window and reminisced about moonlight hikes with our classmates. Memory upon memory crowded our minds and we cherished them together.

I packed Ed's suitcase and my own and the next morning Jean and I headed for the airport. From the plane's window I could see the coffin waiting to be loaded onto the plane.

During the flight God spoke to me, not in an audible voice or in a vision, but with heart-thoughts which I knew were from Him. It was as if He asked, "Are you going to stay home and feel sorry for yourself or are you going on tour to challenge young people to give their lives for Christ's service as Ed gave his?"

I had said to Bob Reed earlier, "Tour is scheduled to begin in a month. I'm not sure I can handle it."

He understood.

"We don't expect you to," he said kindly. "You will be excused."

Our arrival in Dayton was traumatic not only for me but for our son Jim. He had planned a month in advance to come from Texas for a visit on this very day, timing his arrival to coincide with our return from Nyack.

He never saw his father alive but he and Dan mourned and wept together—the first time they had seen each other in 10 years. The girls also came for the funeral—the first time all of us had been together in 16 years.

Now it seemed the Lord was asking me to fulfill the tour assignment. I wanted to obey Him. I checked with my children. I needed their advice. Ruth, a nurse, said the tour would be a wise thing for me to do. The others agreed with her, confirming my own opinion and what I believed to be God's direction.

An intensive month of work followed: probate court, bank visits, preparation of messages and slide presentations. Because Kodak film could not be developed in Israel I had more than 3,000 slides to be scrutinized, labeled and sorted. At two o'clock the morning of the day of departure I was still filling carousels and packing my suitcases.

I will never forget the first Sunday of the tour. The offeratory that morning was "Savior, Like a Shepherd Lead Us," a hymn that had been sung at our wedding. I sat on the platform, my fingernails digging into clenched fists, my teeth clamped tightly, tears trying to force their way down my cheeks.

Lord, help me! I prayed in desperation. And He did.

Nine weeks of traveling and speaking in 18 churches kept me busy and undoubtedly lessened my grieving, though I cried myself to sleep each night. I know people were praying for me and God had wondrous ways of comforting and providing daily help and strength as I leaned on Him for support.

I also knew that God had called *me* to mis-

sionary service and mine was not finished. I
returned to Israel as planned in June, 1985.

24

The Bethlehem Star

A huge, five-pointed star graces the top of the church where the cave of Christ's birth is located. It is lit at night and visible from more than a mile away, shining bright against the dark sky just as that miraculous one did on the first Christmas Eve.

When Jesus' birth was prophesied in Isaiah 9:6, He was assigned five special names: Wonderful, Counselor, The Mighty God, The Everlasting Father, The Prince of Peace. Each of these names has significance as far as the Middle East is concerned.

Wonderful

While a young Jewish couple was doing their two years of mandatory army training following graduation from high school, someone gave them a Bible. They began reading it and gradually became convinced that Jesus was truly their Messiah.

After they finished military service they settled in Beersheba. One day as they walked down the street they saw a sign which read:

Bible House. Inside they found not only Bibles but souvenirs, a lending library, a reading room, new books and a talented manager, Olavi Syvanto.

They talked with Olavi and discovered there were other Jewish believers in the Messiah. They had thought they were the only ones in the whole country of Israel! A few years ago the estimated number of such believers was 400. Today some say it could be as high as 4,000.

Any Jew who publicly declares his or her faith can expect persecution from Jewish extremists: harassing telephone calls, houses broken into, furniture smashed, etc. Yet God is calling out a people for His name. Perhaps even now He is preparing the 144,000 who will be witnesses for Him in the last days.

Wonderful things are happening among the Arabs too.

Before Israel became a nation in 1948, services were held at our large International Church in Jerusalem for Jews and Arabs as well as foreigners. But after Jerusalem was divided by the United Nations, the Arabs could no longer attend the church because it was located in a Jewish area. So they found and rented rooms in the Old City, the West Bank.

The Arab church did not grow. Older Christians died, others fled to Jordan and became part of our congregations there. Still others scattered to Syria where they joined the Damascus church which has mothered many new churches, a *wonderful* story in itself.

But missionaries were faithful in working and praying and God had plans of His own for that little Arab church.

One memorable Sunday I walked into the youth room. I thought of the many years of weekly youth meetings that had been sponsored by missionaries. Now there were 18 empty chairs. My heart ached as I looked at them.

Alone in the building, I sat down on each chair and prayed that God would bring in someone to fill it. There were hundreds of unchurched high school and college-age young people in the immediate vicinity. What we needed was a zealous youth leader to reach them.

During furlough I had repeatedly asked special prayer for this need. I did not know that God's answer was already on the way.

When I returned from furlough I met Roger and Ellen Elbel who had been evacuated from Lebanon because of the war. They were now appointed to work in Jerusalem, and I soon found out that we shared a mutual burden and vision for youth work.

The Elbels had brought with them a newly converted Lebanese refugee named Abraham whom they were discipling. He was the very leader we needed.

We organized a weekly youth Bible study program. Indigenous Arab music was imported

from Egypt and Jordan, and Ellen and I tran-
scribed the melodies and wrote chords. Most
were in the minor key, some worshipful, others
lively. The words were beautiful, many of them
direct quotations from the Scriptures.

Within a few months as many as 24 young
people were attending the meetings and several accepted Christ as Savior. In fact, as the discipling program continued, the young people
caught the vision of leading both their peers
and parents to the Lord. It was a *wonderful*
problem to have to carry in extra chairs on
Sunday mornings, and often people were standing at the door and outside the windows.

One hot afternoon five Arab young people
including Abraham were baptized in the Jordan
River. Nearly 70 persons gathered to join in
the celebration. Some said, "This is the first
baptismal service I have ever seen." Others
asked to be included next time.

And they were. Over a period of four years,
30 young people took the step of baptism and
several went on to attend Bible college.

The 18 chairs? They were more than full!
God was working in a *wonderful* way among the
Arabs.

Counselor

Joseph was born in the Armenian section of
Jerusalem. His ancestors had fled from their
own country when the Turks began persecuting

and murdering their people before and during World War I.

Joseph's mother was a Christian but his father was reluctant to accept evangelical teaching.

One day little Joseph was given permission by his mother to attend a Child Evangelism class taught by a missionary. He was so happy when he learned that Jesus loved him that he wanted to attend the class every week. But his face grew sad and big tears began rolling down his cheeks.

"What's wrong, Joseph?" the teacher asked.

"I'm afraid if my father finds out where I have been he will beat me," Joseph replied. "And he won't let me come to this class again."

"Well, we will pray that your father will not beat you and that he will let you come to our class."

The next week Joseph arrived at class, his face beaming.

"You prayed and my father has let me come!"

From that time on Joseph grew in the Lord. Eventually he married an Arab Christian girl and they became faithful members of the Alliance congregation. Their one disappointment was that after four years of marriage they still had no children, a grievous thing in Mid-East culture.

Joseph had a good job as a jeweler but it was necessary for him to work on Sunday. One day he came to talk with us.

"I want to be able to go to church every Sunday but my Jewish boss refuses to give me even a few hours off. I have promised to work double time, overtime, anything. But the man adamantly refuses."

"Joseph, this is a decision you must make," we replied. "God is your *Counselor*. We will pray with you and for you as you talk this problem over with Him."

A couple of months later Joseph came to tell us that he had quit his job. He set up a little workroom in his home and began to take private orders, which included an Israeli government contract to make insignias for their army uniforms.

Soon Joseph was making twice as much money as he had made working for the Jewish man. And nine months later God blessed his childless marriage with a son!

Joseph was abundantly rewarded for going to God, the ultimate *Counselor*.

The Mighty God

On a blustery winter afternoon I was driving from Bethlehem to Jerusalem to attend a staff prayer meeting. I intended to park at the Anglican International School but when I drove up to the gates I found them locked. I tried my key but for some reason it would not work.

What could I do? It was extremely difficult to find a parking place in Jerusalem, and if I had to search on that maze of one-way streets I would be late for the meeting. In the past six weeks I had already been given four parking tickets! I did not want another one.

"Lord, now what shall I do?" I prayed desperately.

I climbed back into my car and shifted into reverse, ready to back away, when suddenly I saw the gates slowly swinging open!

"Thank You, Lord," I responded happily. I parked quickly, raced down the street, burst through the door of the Alliance Guest Home and shouted to all the missionaries, "Guess what? You know how the Lord sent an angel to deliver Peter from prison and opened the gate for him? Well, He just opened a gate for me!"

The *Mighty God* had opened those heavy gates in response to a prayer of desperation.

The Everlasting Father

Muslims believe that God has 100 names. They say that they know 99 and the camel knows the other. It will not tell anyone what it is and that is why it wears a smirk on its face.

To gain merit for going to heaven religious Muslims may carry a string of 33 beads similar to a rosary. As they finger each bead they repeat one of the names of God—three times around for a total of 99 names. Most of the names are the same ones we attribute to God: merciful, compassionate, holy, faithful, powerful, gracious, infinite, guardian, majestic.

But what is the 100th name of God? I believe it is love, because of all those 99 names not one is love.

The Bible says, "God is love." A Muslim does not know Him as the *Everlasting Father*, the One who truly loves His children. It was this Father of love who had brought us to Israel to share His story.

The Prince of Peace

Riots, demonstrations, curfews, shootings, rock fights, tire burnings and tear gas episodes in the West Bank occurred almost daily. *Would there ever be lasting peace?* people wondered.

We were sitting in a Bedouin tent in the desert. Across the fire sat our elderly host.

"We've been under the rule of four different nations in my lifetime," he said. "The Turks, until the British came in 1918, then the Jordanians and now the Israelis. Yet we do not have peace."

He picked up a pinch of sand between two fingers.

"When we die we can't take this much with us," he said, letting the tiny grains drift to the ground.

"You're right," we agreed. "But we've come with a message of peace for your heart. And this peace you can take with you."

I lived among the Palestinian Arabs on the

West Bank for 15 years and I learned to understand their point of view. Using an acrostic for
the word Peace let me try to explain in a sim-
plified way how an Arab sees things.

The P stands for People and Property.

The major bone of contention between the
Jews and Arabs is land rights. Each group
believes the land belongs to it. The Jews say
God gave the land to them and cite passages in
the Old Testament as proof:

> *"The* LORD *said to Abram after Lot
> had parted from him, 'Lift up your eyes
> from where you are and look north and
> south, east and west. All the land that
> you see I will give to you and your off-
> spring forever. I will make your offspring
> like the dust of the earth, so that if any-
> one could count the dust, then your off-
> spring could be counted. Go, walk
> through the length and breadth of the
> land, for I am giving it to you.'" (Genesis
> 13:14-17)*

But the Arabs argue: Yes, God did give it to
the Jews, but they sinned by worshiping idols,
and God scattered them to the four corners of
the earth. They have returned as it was prophesied, but many of them do not even believe in
God, and those who claim to be religious are
not tolerant of others. In fact, they zealously
persecute Christians. Ironically the Jews seem

more tolerant of Muslims than of Christians.

On one occasion Jewish zealots broke into our meeting place and set it on fire. On a second visit they turned on a hose and ruined the carpet and piano. Crosses in our cemetery have been repeatedly destroyed. Newspaper articles proclaim, "Missions are the cancer of our society. They must be eradicated."

The E in peace stands for Enemies. Jews and Arabs antagonize each other.

A few years ago Jewish young people were polled to determine their attitude toward Arabs. The majority said, "The Arabs are all right; we try to live together in peace."

After the Uprising (see next chapter), a poll revealed a dramatic change in attitude.

"We hate Arabs," the young people admitted.

Without doubt, the feeling is mutual. Why?

The answer an Arab would give is that their property has been confiscated and their beautiful homes taken over by Jews. The Jews have also built settlements on the West Bank and bulldozed roads through Arab vineyards, orchards and olive groves. When the Arabs threw stones in retaliation, the Jews used bullets and tear gas.

Jewish military occupation of the West Bank also gave cause for rebellion. Arabs were subjected to strict, costly and humiliating procedures when crossing the river to visit relatives in Jordan.

In retaliation Arab terrorists frequently

opened fire on Jewish buses, injuring or killing many. Stabbings occur. Bombs are planted in unusual places: a loaf of bread, a package left on a bus or a street corner. No one knows when or where the next explosion might take place.

Jewish terrorists retaliate by hiding bombs on Arab buses. Vigilantes fire at passing Arab cars or crowds of people at a bus stop. The pendulum swings back and forth, each time more viciously than the last.

Who is right? Who is wrong? When two factions are fighting and each has legitimate causes, how can the problem be resolved?

The A in peace represents Arms, Armies, Aid and Agreements.

Israel has one of the toughest and most efficient armies in the world. The IDF (Israeli Defense Force) patrols all borders as well as the streets of villages and cities in the West Bank.

Presidents Carter, Begin and Sadat signed an agreement to return the Sinai Peninsula to Egypt in exchange for peace, but the result was only tenuous at best.

The Jerusalem Post's cartoon called "Dry Bones" pictured two Jews talking: "When the American Secretary of State comes to try and make peace, he'll have just two little problems."

"Oh? And what might those be?" the other asks.

"Well, the Jews won't listen to him. And the Arabs won't talk to him." Such is the impasse of international diplomacy.

Some say that American aid to Israel totals the equivalent of approximately $100 per person per year (this figure may be underestimated; others say it is closer to $1,000) and there are over four million Jews in Israel. This financial support, whatever the amount may be, antagonizes the Arabs. They declare with irony, "America is right in the middle of Jerusalem. Jer-USA-lem."

What then is the answer?

Christ and His Cross—the C in peace.

Palestinian Arab Christians, dear friends of ours, frequently invited us to Sunday dinner in their home. There we met a Jewish believer in the Messiah who had a standing invitation to the same home for the weekly feast. A Jew and an Arab eating together in Christian fellowship? Yes, they were one in Christ.

Our Palestinian Arab Alliance young people were invited to sing at a Jewish youth retreat. Arab and Jewish youth meeting together in love? Yes, brought together by the love of Christ.

Christ is the only one who can bridge the gulf of hatred, revenge and retaliation. He alone is the Prince of Peace.

The last E in peace brings us to the End. Ezekiel, Daniel and Revelation picture the events as they will occur. Of particular interest and significance in our day is the prophesied rebuilding of the temple on the Mount of Olives.

A few years ago archaeologists digging underneath the temple mount in Jerusalem found ruins thought to belong to Solomon's temple. This discovery altered the views of many Bible scholars who once believed the Jews must rebuild their temple on the site of the gold Dome of the Rock, the second most holy place of Muslim worship.

Now, with the ruins not under the Muslim mosque as had been supposed but beside it, the way could be paved for someone to mediate between the Jews and Arabs. The Muslims could keep their mosque and the Jews could rebuild their temple on its original site.

Such a compromise might bring about peace and the mediator would be hailed as the great peacemaker—the messiah for whom both Jews and Muslims wait. (Even as this book was in the final preparation stages, PLO leader Yasser Arafat and Israeli prime minister Yitzhak Rabin signed a major but controversial peace agreement in Washington, D.C.)

According to the Bible, however, after three and one-half years this messiah will declare himself to be God and will sit in the temple demanding to be worshiped. But he will not be *the* Messiah—he will be the Antichrist. And his peace will be false.

Jesus Christ, the true Prince of Peace, has promised to return. Until then, His peace fills the heart of anyone—Jew or Gentile—who follows Him.

25

The Uprising

It was 1988. A bright red sticker was pasted on the package that came from the post office: "Be Careful! Dear Citizen, for your security, don't open this parcel before checking. Are you expecting a parcel from this address? If you have any doubt, please advise the employee who will call the police for aid. The Ministry of Communication."

Boobytrapped parcels. Shootings in the middle of the night. Bullets flying. Ambulance sirens screaming. Oil slicks purposely placed on the roads. All of these were part of what became known as The Uprising—a sudden escalation of what had been sporadic outbursts by the Palestinians that had been occurring ever since Israel became a nation in 1948.

One morning my doorbell rang at five o'clock. I was greeted by armed Israeli soldiers.

"You have graffiti painted on your front wall. Get it off by 12 o'clock. We will return to check."

I phoned my landlord and by seven a.m. he had spray-painted out the offending slogans. Eventually there was so much graffiti throughout the neighborhood and so many colors of paint on top of each other that the soldiers could not keep up with it.

Pictures of the green, white, black and red Palestinian flag and slogans of, "There is no god but Allah," "Palestine," "The Uprising," "No Jews," adorned walls and doors in many areas of the West Bank.

Stores were closed several days a week due to curfews imposed by the Israeli army or strikes called by one or more Muslim factions. Shelves lay as bare as Mother Hubbard's cupboard because Jewish merchants were afraid their delivery vehicles would be stoned.

It was difficult to get to town, and sometimes the moneylender's office where we got our checks cashed was closed when I did get there.

Stonings were followed by shootings, stabbings by beatings, broken bones and death.

One Sunday morning after a church service, a few of us were standing outside in the sun drinking tea when we saw smoke coming from an area close by. A slight breeze was blowing and before we realized what was happening we were inhaling tear gas.

We rushed into the church but one of the ladies who was crippled froze in panic. I hurried outside to get her a drink of water. I could barely see. My nose, mouth and throat felt like they were on fire. I nearly passed out. Headache and nausea followed.

Then just when it seemed safe to leave the

church, a bomb was thrown. I waited a while longer and finally left to visit one of our church members who lived nearby. Another bomb exploded while I was there. We later learned that nearly 200 Arab women and girls had been shouting and stoning Jewish soldiers. The tear gas was used to disperse the rioters.

On another occasion a funeral procession went by the church carrying the open coffin of a young man who had been killed by Israeli gunfire. The pallbearers and crowd following in the narrow street angrily shouted slogans. We locked the church door and kept still until they passed.

About three hours later soldiers began firing in the street outside the church. People ran helter-skelter. Roger Elbel looked out the window and saw an Israeli soldier lying unconscious, his head bleeding. Other soldiers came and carried him away on a stretcher.

The news spread that one of our own young men had been involved in the incident and arrested along with his brother. They lived in the same compound as the dead youth's family. Soldiers located the neighborhood, beat our young man and took him for questioning.

Later we learned that the young Palestinian victim had been standing at an Arab bus stop along with other people. A car of Jewish civilians came along and opened fire, killing the 17-year-old and wounding many others.

The trouble continued. The next day there

was more shooting and the smell of tear gas still lingered in the air. Fist-sized rocks had smashed windows in the neighborhood and glass lay everywhere.

The Arabs were incensed because the Israelis wanted to do an autopsy on the young man who had been killed. The family refused and smuggled his body out of the hospital. One rumor said the Muslims took him to the mosque because he was a martyr. Another reported that during the procession the corpse fell out of the coffin onto the ground and had to be put back. He was quickly buried before Jewish soldiers could whisk him away.

I visited the home of our Arab young man who was implicated. His sister remarked, "This is slow death. They [the Jews] are killing us." My heart ached.

>―◆>―O―<◆―<

It was a cold, rainy winter evening. One of our Palestinian young men was on his way home from work. He lived in the Old City of Jerusalem and was passing through one of its gates guarded by Jewish soldiers. They grabbed him, made him sit down on the wet pavement and beat him. When they checked his ID they saw that he was a Christian.

"What does your Bible tell you to do if you are hit on one cheek?" they taunted, slapping him on the side of the face.

Then they smacked him on the other cheek. Someone who knew the young man came along and vouched for his good character, explaining that he was not a terrorist. The soldiers let him go.

He came to church that evening and told his story with tears in his eyes, his lips trembling. He ended by saying, "I know that I must pray for my enemies." He and 15 other Palestinian young people got down on their knees and prayed for the Jews.

The China Post on Wednesday, March 3, 1993 reported that "the death [of an Israeli who drove into a Palestinian refugee camp] raised to 116 the number of Israelis killed in the more than five-year-old Palestinian Uprising. Israelis have killed 1,023 Palestinians in that time."

>━┼━◆━○━◆┼━◄

I decided to have a monthly tea to which I would invite my neighbors. To make it attractive I planned to include various demonstrations such as cake decorating, flower arranging, crafts, etc.

The women came—a whole living room full. To begin our first meeting I suggested we sing and proceeded to hand out chorus books. The response was candidly negative.

"What have we got to sing about?" one woman asked.

I understood the bitterness in her voice. The Uprising was in progress. These women carried heavy burdens. Their hearts ached. They had no joy.

Families were suffering financially. Jobs were

scarce in the West Bank. With the decline of tourism, souvenir shops lacked business. Men who had been making good wages found themselves unable to provide adequate food, clothes and shelter for their dependents.

Arabs are a proud race. I came across this poetic revelation in a third grade Arabic reader from the Jordanian Department of Education: "My tribe, my root, my ancestry, my lineage, is my glory, my honor, my hiding place if I'm afraid; My javelin, my shield, my sword if I'm angry." These proud Arabs felt demeaned, humiliated.

The Uprising also affected their social life. Schools were frequently closed due to demonstrations. Some students lost an entire year of classes.

Marriages had to be postponed because of lack of funds as well as job training and housing.

The political situation also caused devastating emotional reactions even among children. A 12-year-old girl remarked, "My heart is full of poison." Her brother and other close relatives had been killed.

Because of the constant fighting many women lived in fear. When would Jewish soldiers knock on their door in the middle of the night and drag a husband or son or father off to prison?

These financial, emotional and political burdens weighed heavily on the hearts of the Arab women.

But they also carried spiritual burdens. Muslims and nominal Christians believe they must earn the right to enter heaven by doing good works. Nominal Christians should give money to the church, support the priests, help those in need. Muslims must obey their five-pillared creed: repeat the oath that there is no god but Allah, pray five times a day, give alms to the poor, fast one month of the year and go on a pilgrimage to Mecca.

Superstition is mixed with tradition. A lamb is killed to ensure good luck in building a house or protect a car against accident. Crossed-eyes are stuck on the back bumper of a car to ward off bad luck or possibly curses.

A Muslim woman fears three things: divorce, demons and death. If she does not please her husband and especially if she is childless, he has the privilege of saying "I divorce you" three times. If that happens she must leave and return to her father or brother or other male relative who will look after her.

Demons are believed to inhabit jackals, hyenas and owls at night. We sat in the home of a well-educated young woman far out in the wilderness of Judea. Over a cup of tea we discussed the Bible and the Koran. "I'm afraid of the dark, of the demons," she confessed.

Death holds no promise for a Muslim. When he dies he must walk a hairline bridge over hell. An angel perches on each shoulder. If his good deeds outweigh his bad the good angel will lead him by the hand across the bridge and into paradise. But if his bad deeds outweigh the good, the bad angel will push him off the bridge into hell.

Added to the sadness of their lives there is no assurance of sins forgiven and hope of eternal life in heaven.

It was understandable, then, that my neighbor women in Bethlehem felt there was little cause to sing.

They had not read God's promise: ". . . and the ransomed of the LORD will return. They will enter Zion with singing; everlasting joy will crown their heads. Gladness and joy will overtake them, and sorrow and sighing will flee away" (Isaiah 35:10).

26

A Gold-toothed Sheik

Rarely in all the years Ed and I visited in the desert did we meet opposition. Bedouin tradition requires that hospitality be shown to any visitor. Even an enemy must be welcomed and protected for three days. But one day as we drove through the mountains of Judea in the area of Toccoa, a van overtook us and stopped. A man got out and came to our car.

"Don't you ever come to my tribe again!" he shouted angrily in Ed's face. "The Bible you left with us last year I tore up and burned. If you ever come here again I'll make trouble for you."

We were shocked. This certainly was the exception rather than the rule. When the sheik finished his tirade, my wise and patient husband quietly answered, "God loves you."

This was a new concept to the Muslim who knew God as the One who decrees punishment for doing wrong but not as a loving Father. The sheik was speechless. He turned and climbed back into his van and drove away.

A few years later some Nyack College students were taking their winter term in Jerusalem

and asked me to accompany them on Bedouin
evangelism. I prayed about where we should go,
and when they arrived at my apartment in
Bethlehem, I explained that I felt we should go
to the valley of Toccoa.

"We may be like Daniel going into the lions'
den," I said, explaining our previous encounter
with the sheik, "but I believe this is where the
Lord is directing us."

We prayed together and started out. It was a
15-mile drive through the wilderness of Judea.
Wild crimson anemones were pushing up
through the rocky terrain. The sun was glorious
and on one high hill we could look across to
the misty blue-gray of the Dead Sea.

The first black goat-and-camel-hair tent stood
slightly off the road. We parked and a Bedouin
woman came to welcome us.

"Peace to you," we greeted her in Arabic.
She invited us for coffee and we had an enjoy-
able visit with a group of relatives who gathered. The young people gave their testimonies
and I translated for them. We presented the
family with a Bible as our way of thanking
them for their hospitality. Then with the formal
expression, "May God increase your wealth,"
we left.

After visiting another family we decided to
turn back because it was getting late. Just as we
came parallel with the first tent, there in the
middle of the road stood a Bedouin. I stopped
the car.

"You must come and visit me," he said.

"We already visited your tent," I replied.

"Well, I was not here," he answered brusquely. "I've been away and I've just come back. I'm the chief of this tribe."

When I heard that I knew we must not offend him so we got out of the car and followed him to the tent. He was extremely gracious and ordered coffee for us.

Then he smiled. When I saw his gold tooth I knew immediately who he was. This was the same sheik who had threatened Ed and me a few years earlier. Now we were sitting in his home! On furlough I had asked Christians to pray for the gold-toothed sheik in the valley of Toccoa. Someone had prayed and God was answering!

Suddenly during the conversation the sheik looked at me from across the fire.

"Haven't I seen you somewhere before?" he asked.

Not wanting to rehearse the earlier incident, I quickly changed the subject. Thankfully, he did not press for an answer.

I learned that the sheik's three-week-old grandson was in the hospital just down the road from my apartment. I promised to visit him and to bring word to the family. This was the beginning of a lasting friendship between us.

The last time I went to Toccoa I could not locate my friend's tent. I inquired in the area and finally found his wife.

"Where is your husband?" I asked when he didn't appear.

"He's dead," she answered soberly.

What a shock! How thankful I was that he had heard the gospel and had the opportunity of accepting Christ as his Savior. I will be looking for the gold-toothed sheik from the valley of Toccoa in heaven.

27

A Camel Safari

"How would you like to take a camel trip in the desert of Sinai?" I asked a group of young people in our Arab Alliance church in Jerusalem. Their eyes lit up with pleasure and anticipation as I explained that our purpose would be to reach Bedouins with the gospel.

When my husband died, several memorial gifts were sent for the Bedouin work. Now, after much prayer, I felt that financing this trip to Sinai where we had carried on a "Bibles for Bedouins" program for several years was an appropriate way to use those funds.

But first we had to get through a vast amount of red tape. The four young people were Palestinian Arabs with neither Israeli nor Jordanian passports. By the time we learned they needed special travel documents, which normally take two weeks to obtain, we were only four days from our scheduled departure. Impossibility number one.

Repeatedly the Lord said, "Trust Me." So I did. And the night before we were to leave the papers came!

We tossed sleeping bags, canteens and a change of clothes together with a number of Arabic Bibles into the van and headed south.

It took the entire next day to cross the border. Israeli officials were reluctant to let Palestinian Arabs leave, and the Egyptian officials were just as reluctant to let them enter. Our identification papers were carefully scrutinized, and the new travel documents we had just obtained were declared useless.

We went to the Egyptian consulate in Elat but were flatly refused permission to enter the country. The consul himself adamantly declared, "Impossible. It's never been done."

I had warned the young people to keep calm and pray. We did not argue or shout or demand our rights but sat quietly and waited to see what God would do.

I had read Romans 10:11, "No one who believes in him shall be disappointed" (Weymouth), so when it looked hopeless I whispered, "Lord, I'm getting disappointed!"

Again the Lord said, "Trust Me." By the end of the day God had changed the consul's mind, and soon his aides delivered specially drawn-up papers into our hands. Impossibility number two!

Finally at 10 p.m. we arrived at a Bedouin camp half way down the Sinai Peninsula. We were tired and hungry. We had not eaten since our lunch of hamburgers and fries at McDavid's in Elat.

We found a little bamboo restaurant beside the Red Sea and woke up the proprietor who fixed dinner for us. By midnight I had managed to arrange for a string of camels to be ready in the morning.

Early the next day the six of us—Roger Elbel, the four Palestinian young people and I—climbed onto our camels and headed down a road beside the beautiful Red Sea. The water gently rippled in colors from deep blue to turquoise. Leaving the road, we "comfortably walked" and "miserably trotted" across scorching, sandy wasteland and up rocky valleys between stark, stony mountains.

My unruly camel refused to obey the driver's prodding stick and became so violently angry that it bent its long neck around, opened its flabby lips revealing a cavernous mouth filled with huge, dirty teeth and aimed those teeth directly at my leg. Within an inch of being bitten I moved back quickly and was glad to slide off until the beast could be brought back under control.

We stopped at an oasis for lunch. Two girls from New Zealand had also come to the oasis by camel. One of our young men talked with them and led them to the Lord. A third exciting and unexpected blessing!

That evening at a restaurant built of palm branches and bamboo poles, we reclined on colorful striped rugs around a central platter and ate a supper of delicious charcoal-roasted chicken.

After the meal we, along with the sheik in whose room we were staying, sat out on the sand around a fire where several other Bedouins had gathered.

One of our young men played the accordion. We sang and the audience applauded appreciatively. Three young people gave brief testimonies and then a red-haired girl, recently converted, talked from her heart for nearly half an hour. All the while the sheik smiled his approval.

Finally she asked, "Now who would like to pray?"

My heart nearly burst with joy as I watched the sheik himself and another Bedouin open their arms in an attitude of surrender to God and move their lips in prayer. We gave Bibles to each one and returned to our room walking not on sand but on air.

"What next?" asked the young people excitedly. "We can't stop now." So instead of staying in the room, we went back to the bamboo restaurant, and there our zealous little redhead led the Egyptian owner to the Lord!

What a trip! Miracle after miracle. God had used each of our young people in a special way—negotiating with officials, singing and playing, witnessing.

I thought of Ed in heaven. He must have been rejoicing with the angels when those Bedouins prayed, for theirs was the first response we had seen in 10 years of evangelism among them.

". . . unless a kernel of wheat falls to the ground and dies, it remains only a single seed. But if it dies, it produces many seeds" (John 12:24).

The Burden of the Desert

"An oracle concerning the Desert by the Sea . . . (Isaiah 21:1a).

Blazing sun beats relentlessly
upon thorny little acacia trees, stunted shrubs.
Scorching wind carves sand into precise, rippled designs,
smoothes high dunes into slopes like ski slides,
scatters tumbleweed aimlessly.
Dust devils whirl and cavort.
Mirages beckon temptingly.
Terrible majesty!

Camels plod toward a black goat-hair tent
tucked into a valley.
Beside the road lies a headload of spindly sticks
gathered and tied into a bundle by a Bedouin woman.
Her face is hidden under a heavy veil of coins and beads,
but her dark eyes are beautiful and expressive.

She asks for water.
Like the desert, she is thirsty.

We open our guarded supply
and pour it freely into her cupped
* hands.*
She offers "a thousand thanks,"
gratefulness reflected in her eyes.

The mirage of her faith promises par-
* adise,*
so she follows it hopefully.
But her spiritual thirst is not slaked.
She does not know if she will inherit
* eternal life,*
for she has no "blessed assurance";
she has not tasted "love divine."

Then we share with her God's abun-
* dant*
water of life in Christ
that she may drink her fill,
for her soul lies parched and barren.
Like the desert, she is thirsty.

—Virginia Jacober

28

The Promise

"How would you like to go to India?" Bob Reed asked as we sat at our headquarters office in Jerusalem.

Return to India? I could not believe my ears!

I had gone back to Bethlehem after Ed died but a clergy visa had not been issued. My tourist permit expired every three months and it could only be renewed up to two years. Wanting to abide by Israeli rules, we knew the time had come for me to leave the country "for a reasonable length of time."

As soon as the possibility of going to India was suggested, through my mind flashed the promise God had given me when we left India: "I am with you and will watch over you wherever you go, and I will bring you back to this land" (Genesis 28:15). Was God really going to take me back to the "other land" I loved? My heart nearly burst with joy and anticipation.

There were no diplomatic relations between India and Israel. This meant I would have to obtain an entry visa from a different country. It was a long and complicated process and more than once I held my breath and prayed as I waited to see how God would keep His promise.

I finally arrived in Bombay. It was 1988—15 years after I had been given that comforting promise. Ed and Ruth Lewellen and I headed up country to Ahmedabad for the silver anniversary of our radio work. Elmer and Muriel Entz met us at the train station. We dashed to their home, changed into our saris and hurried to the church, arriving just in time for the service.

Myriads of memories flooded my mind as I sat in silent reverie admiring the bright decorations and enjoying the orchestral prelude. All of a sudden I heard the master of ceremonies announce, "Mrs. Jacober will open our meeting with prayer."

I had not prayed in the Gujarati language for 15 years!

"Oh Lord," I breathed in desperation, "help me!" I stood up and somehow He did help me and the words began to flow.

During those three months of March, April and May, which I called "hot, hotter, hottest," many things looked familiar: littered streets, masses of people—some still living and sleeping on sidewalks, gutters used as latrines, blaring horns, blazing sun, banyan trees, raucous cawing of crows, tasty bananas and mangoes, gorgeous saris in rainbow colors, the scent of incense and jasmine, temple bells and the Gujarati language which was like sweet music to my ears!

But there were many changes: photocopiers, computers, TVs and videos. Bicycles had been replaced by thousands of motor scooters. Modern shops displayed a wide variety of imported products. Comfortable air-conditioned train coaches replaced the decrepit ones we had been used to riding.

But the most thrilling change was in the growth of our Alliance work: 17 new churches had been established bringing the total to 86. Indian Christians had caught the vision of supporting these projects voluntarily as their service to the Lord, and they were now taking places of leadership. The months passed all too quickly.

On the return flight to Jerusalem our plane had engine trouble and we were delayed at an Arabian desert oasis. I spent much of the time chatting with an Italian construction engineer in the next seat.

"They are all good," he said, referring to the religions of the world, "and they all lead to God."

I had heard that many times and responded forcefully.

"Max," I said, "you need a heart love and relationship to God."

My answer caught him by surprise.

"You are the first person who ever told me that!" he admitted.

This opporunity to speak with Max was worth the six planes, a lost suitcase (later miraculously found) and seven days travel. And best of all, it was all part of God's plan.

God had kept His promise. He had brought me back to "the land." My heart could rest.

29

Bedouins in Heaven

*"The desert tribes will bow before
him . . ." (Psalm 72:9)*

*"After this I looked and there before me
was a great multitude that no one could
count, from every nation, tribe, people
and language, standing before the throne
and in front of the Lamb. They were
wearing white robes and were holding
palm branches in their hands.*

*Then one of the elders asked me, 'These
in white robes—who are they, and where
did they come from?'*

I answered, 'Sir, you know.'

*And he said, 'These are they who have
come out of the great tribulation; they
have washed their robes and made them
white in the blood of the Lamb.*

Therefore,

*'They are before the throne of God
    and serve him day and night in his
        temple;
and he who sits on the throne will*

spread his tent over them.
Never again will they hunger;
never again will they thirst.
The sun will not beat upon them,
nor any scorching heat.
For the Lamb at the center of the throne
will be their shepherd;
he will lead them to springs of living
water.
And God will wipe away every tear from
their eyes.' " *(Revelation 7:9, 13-17)*

Their spotless white robes and headdresses blow in the breeze as they stride purposefully toward the throne of God. They bow with the angels, their heads touching the golden floor of heaven. It is a humble position they were accustomed to on earth, one of respect for God. They are fulfilling the promise in Psalm 72:9: "The desert tribes will bow before him."

They are no longer suffering from disease or sickness. There are no blind, deaf, dumb or lame Bedouins here. No heart attacks from the pressure of raising money to send their sons abroad for an education or from receiving news from the Israeli army that a son is missing in action or has been wounded or killed.

No tents to be laboriously woven by the women, put up or taken down, because "he who sits on the throne will spread his tent over them."

No camel to be rounded up, brought in from

the desert, watered and loaded with all their possessions to move on in search of fresh pasture for their flocks. There is no need to depend on livestock for food. A Kingly Shepherd now leads them as they did their own sheep.

No more scrounging in the scorching heat of the desert for firewood to cook meals or boil coffee or sweet tea. No need to mix flour and water to bake paper-thin wheat bread over hot coals. The family will never be hungry because the Lamb, the Bread of Heaven, will feed them.

No more water to be carried from the nearest well in a goatskin or jar or poured into plastic containers and tied to a donkey, because Christ shall lead them to springs of living water and their thirst will be quenched.

No lamb to be slain as a sacrifice and its blood sprinkled on the foundation of a house or smeared on a camel's neck or on the fender of a new car to ensure good luck. A holy man need not be intreated to mediate with God for flocks or family. Christ did all this for them long ago.

No more grieving over the death of a family member, an unhappy marriage or instant divorce. No fighting or court cases to be reviewed by the appointed sheiks. No punishment or prison sentences to be meted out. Theirs is peace—perfect peace—for the Prince of Peace reigns in glorious majesty.

Will that gold-toothed sheik from Toccoa be among those who bow before the throne?

The deaf and dumb first wife who wanted so desperately to have the message of the Wordless Book explained to her?

The woman from the rocky wilderness of Judea whose beautiful smile showed she understood the message?

The father who played his one-stringed instrument and sang as we sat in his desert tent?

The young fisherman from the shores of the Red Sea who had been waiting for God's Word for a long, long time?

The two men in Sinai who responded to our fiery little redhead's testimony by extending their hands in prayer?

The dear little humpbacked woman whose son drew a cross in the sand with his finger to point out how Jesus died for her?

The young woman whose veil of coins glittered in the sun while toddlers tugged at her skirts?

The children will surely be there: the young boy who stopped his donkey to show us where his father's tent had been moved and sat cross-legged as we told the story of the Good Shepherd; the little girl who picked up shells along the Red Sea to trade for a New Testament; the shepherd boy who played his flute as he tended his flocks; the teenager who caught the goat and milked it to enhance our tea.

And there are more: the woman who gave us a dozen eggs wrapped in her veil in exchange for the Bible we gave her; a donkey driver who traded a handful of cucumbers; the farmer who climbed his palm tree and cut a cluster of dates for us; the truck driver who kissed the Bible we offered; the women to whom we gave medicine and explained that Jesus is the Great Physician; the hungry traveler who asked for bread and received the message that Christ is the Bread of Life; the young goat-herds whose thirst we quenched with our supply of water—both physical and spiritual.

Will they be there?

By faith I believe some from each of the 15 Bedouin tribes will be in heaven, bowing their faces before the throne and worshiping the Lamb shouting,

> *"Salvation belongs to our God,*
> *who sits on the throne,*
> *and to the Lamb. Amen!*
>
> *Praise and glory*
> *and wisdom and thanks and honor*
> *and power and strength*
> *be to our God for ever and ever.*
> *Amen!" (7:10b, 12)*

And to their praises I will add, "Amen and Amen! He is worthy to be praised, for He is a faithful God, a God who keeps His promises."

Epilogue

Virginia Jacober officially retired in 1990 after 41 years of service with The Christian and Missionary Alliance.

But that was not the end of her missionary career. The Mission asked her to return to Jerusalem to manage the guest home, and she served there until an emergency hip replacement necessitated her return to the States.

While she was recovering she wrote this book, and then promptly volunteered her help in churches in Taiwan and Australia.

"I love every minute of these new and challenging experiences," wrote Virginia, "and I plan to continue serving wherever the Lord can use me."

As they say, "Once a missionary, always a missionary."

>−·−◆−·−O−··−◆−·−<

The Jacober children are scattered: Ruth and her family live in Colorado. Dan and his wife are temporarily in India where he is a chemical engineer with the Dupont Corporation. Jim, a bachelor, lives in Dallas, Texas, and Beth and her husband, a missionary kid from Brazil, have three children and live in Alabama.

Bibliography

Dubois, Abbe J.A. *Hindu Manners, Customs and Ceremonies*. Translated from author's French manuscript by Henry K. Beauchamp. Published by Oxford at the Clarendon Press, 3rd edition. London E.C. 4, 1906, 8th reprint 1953.

Stephen, B. "The Rat Temple," *The Enquirer*. Gujarat, India.

Whitney, Anna Temple. "The Kneeling Camel," *The Best Loved Poems of the American People*," pp. 363, 364. Compiled and selected by Hazel Fellerman. Garden City, N.Y.: Doubleday & Co. 1936.

Kirschen. "Dry Bones," *The Jerusalm Post*. Jerusalem, Israel.

_____. "The Temple Mount," *Biblical Archeology Review*, March-April, 1983.

Sevener, Harold A. "The Temple? Where Did It Stand, Where Will It Be Rebuilt?," *The Chosen People*, November 1992 (Part I) and December 1992 (Part II).

Rabinovich, Abraham. "Second Temple, Third Temple, Fourth Temple . . .," *Weekend Magazine*, February 2, 1990, *The Jerusalem Post*.

_____. *The Third Arabic Reader*. Department of Education, Jordan.

Bailey, Clinton. "The Bedouin—People of the Desert," The Holy Land. Palphot Ltd.

_____ Article: *The China Post*, March 3, 1993, Taipei, Taiwan.

DATE DUE